Debt Destroyer

A Proven Plan to Get Out of Debt, Make Money Online & Achieve Financial Freedom

Charlie Johnson

Copyright © 2017 Charlie Johnson

All rights reserved.

Disclaimer

All attempts have been made to verify the information in this book; however, neither the author nor the publisher assumes any responsibility for errors, omissions, or contrary interpretations of the content within.

This book is for entertainment purposes only, and so the views of the author should not be taken as expert instruction or commands. The reader is responsible for his or her own actions.

I am not an accountant or a financial adviser, and nothing in these materials is intended as professional advice. To obtain advice as to the financial, tax, or legal consequence of any action covered in these materials, or any action that you might consider based on these materials, you should consult a financial adviser, an accountant, or both.

Neither the author nor the publisher assumes any responsibility or liability on behalf of the purchaser or reader of this book.

Buyer Bonus

As a way of saying thank you for your purchase, I'm offering a FREE download that's exclusive to my book readers.

It's a Companion Guide that includes all the templates, resources, and tools you'll need to complete the steps in this book – and I put everything together so that you can simply download it, add in your information, and move forward.

These are the EXACT same templates I used to help me pay off $25,000 of debt in four months.

All you have to do is follow the steps.

Go to the Link Below to Download Your Debt Destroyer Companion Guide Now

---------- www.debtdestroyerbook.com/step1 ----------

Dedication

This book is dedicated to all the hard-working Debt Destroyers out there actively striving to achieve financial freedom. By going against the grain and pushing the limits, you inspire the rest of us to fight harder to accomplish our goals. You've all taught me so much about money, motivation, and perseverance, and because of you, my understanding of the word "grit" is forever changed. This book is also dedicated to my friends and family members who supported me while I was paying off my debt, and then again later when I wrote this book. Dave, David, Derek, Joe, Nick, Chris, Brett, and Maddy – thank you all. I'm grateful for your support.

Mom and Dad – Thank you for not flipping out TOO much when you discovered I was sleeping in the woods.

Emily – Thank you for pushing me to write this book.

Contents

Debt Destroyer

Disclaimer

Buyer Bonus

Dedication

Contents

FAQ – Read This First

My Story and Why You Need This Book

How to Use This Book

How to Destroy Your Debt

Part I: The Winner's Mindset

What Kind of Life Do You Want?

Light the Fire: Bullet-Proof Resilience and Limitless Motivation

System Reset: Escaping Paralysis and Igniting Rocket Fuel

Part II: Your Money Framework

Burn Your Ships: Failure is NOT an Option

Figure Out Where You Stand: The Debt Tracker

Taking Massive Action: Airbnb and Sleeping in the Woods

Take Control: A 5 Minute Spending Plan

Where to Start: A 3 Minute Debt Elimination System

Part III: Incredible Profitability

Everything Popular is Wrong: Save Money Like Warren Buffett

Winning the Money Game: Naming Porn Flicks and Selling Restaurants

Sprint or Marathon: A Word of Caution

Action Steps and Guiding Principles

Your Next Step

Can You Do Me a Favor?

About the Author

FAQ – Read This First

Why should I read this book?

I wrote this book to get you out of debt as quickly and as painlessly as possible. I want you to stop worrying about money and get on with your life.

I've been there.

I know how much it sucks to lay awake at night worrying about a mountain of debt hanging over your head, wondering if there's some financial Judgment Day coming when it will finally all come crashing down (and for a long time I didn't even know how big that "mountain" was – I was too afraid to check my accounts and find out).

I also know how to get out.

I erased $25,000 in debt in just 4 months. Just as importantly, I learned how to take control of my finances so that I can do the things I really care about. Now I can afford to spend two months volunteering with orangutans in Borneo, or take a trip to Indonesia to climb an active volcano.

Now that my money situation is under control, I've been traveling the world non-stop for the past 9 months. I started writing this book in Bali, continued working on it in Vietnam, and now I'm putting the finishing touches on it from my office in Spain.

I can show you how to deal with your debt – faster than you probably think is possible – and how to have some fun along the way. After all, this is your life. Shouldn't you enjoy it?

What am I going to learn from this book?

The steps in this book draw on a combination of behavior change science, social psychology, and my own personal experience battling debt, to give you the fastest, most effective plan for paying off your debt and living a life of financial abundance.

This book is about results. I don't care what you "should" be doing – we all know what we "should" do. Stop going out. Learn how to budget. Hoard stacks of coupons like a financially responsible chipmunk preparing for 10 years of winter.

There's only one problem: None of that works! We're human. You can make yourself miserable by cutting back on the things you love, and it'll work… for a little while.

But eventually, you'll snap back like an overstretched rubber band and return to the way things were – and you'll feel worse for having tried and failed.

I wrote this book so that you can follow the steps inside and start getting results right away. My goal is NOT to educate you on how different types of debt work, or the ins and outs of interest rates or loan consolidation.

If you're looking for that type of information, look elsewhere.

Those answers can be found quickly on Google, but will take you down a rabbit-hole of click-baity articles and self-promoting blog posts. If you simply want to read about debt, don't bother with this book. This book is for people who want to take action.

We've been told over and over that there's a lack of financial literacy in our country – and it's true, but it's also not the real problem.

We all know what we need to do at a fundamental knowledge level: Spend less, save more, earn more. That's obvious. The hard part is making small, consistent, POWERFUL changes in our lives that make wealth generation natural and easy.

This book will show you how to do that.

Do I have to sacrifice and become a "money monk"?

Not a chance. This book is NOT about penny pinching and clipping coupons. Instead, I recommend you leverage the power of prioritized spending (more on this in Chapter 9).

By spending on the handful of things that truly matter for your personal happiness and life satisfaction (so you can enjoy the present) and cutting back on everything else (so you have money to enjoy the future), you can dramatically improve your cash flow while still being able to travel, eat well, or do whatever else it is that makes life meaningful for you right now.

Will I have to learn a bunch of complicated techniques?

No. To be honest, there isn't anything that complicated about paying off debt. Financial "gurus" and so called money "experts" might have you believe otherwise (it's how they get paid), but the truth is that the real challenge of paying off debt and building wealth has nothing to do with secret formulas, silver bullet methods, or investment algorithms.

If those "tricks" were the path to wealth, then it would take the burden of responsibility off YOU – because how could you possibly build wealth when you don't have those tricks in your back pocket, right?

The truth is simpler than that, but harder to hear. The TRUE challenge of achieving debt freedom and building wealth is picking a strategy and sticking with it.

The solution? Use a simple plan that gets you tangible results fast (so you will stay motivated) while making the hard work easier to digest (so you won't give up). This is that plan.

Do I need to be good with math to be good with money?

I hate to admit it... but I cheated in most of my math classes in high school, and I did everything possible to talk my way out of them in college.

Being good with money is 80% behavior and 20% knowledge – and that knowledge doesn't include equations, calculations, or math problems. Technology does the mental heavy lifting for us these days anyway.

Not to make an ass out of you and me, but I assume you either have a smartphone or a computer, and if you don't, you can always go to a public library to access the internet.

Throughout this book I link to several tools and spreadsheets that you can use for free. They'll handle any calculations that might come up. All you need to do is follow the steps. No math required.

Are you even qualified to be talking about debt?

I want to be 100% transparent about this – I am not a certified anything.

I don't have a fancy finance degree, I've never worked in the industry, and I've never taken a financial literacy class. So why should you listen to what I have to say?

Because I paid off $25,000 of debt in 4 months.

Credit card debt, 20%+ interest rates, medical bills, late IRS payments, getting contacted by creditors – I've been there, it's horrible.

And while there are many paths out of debt, some of them are much faster than others.

Sleeping in the woods, naming porn flicks, selling restaurants... for four months, I tried anything and everything in my quest to pay off debt faster. Some of my experiments were a waste of time, while others paid off like gangbusters – one time I even had to call my bank in order for them to approve an exceptionally large deposit.

Just recently I founded the Boston Debt Destroyers, a group that meets to share personal struggles and trade debt hacking tips. Many of the strategies and tools I'll share with you originated in this debt destroying think tank.

I'm not telling you all this to gloat or show off, but to give you a sense of where I'm coming from and to illustrate what is possible. Someone once told me, "You're not like those financial advisors who learned how to make money by advising people about money. You're like me: someone who wanted to get out of debt fast and just went and did it."

And that's just it. I never planned on any of this happening. I never wanted to learn about how to get out of debt fast. I simply found myself in a position where I needed to get results quickly.

Necessity is the mother of invention.

How fast can I realistically expect to pay off my debt?

I've seen people pay off $52K in seven months, or $25K in four. Obviously, your "Debt Free Date" will depend on a few factors – like your income, and how much debt you have at the moment – but the most important factor is YOU.

You = your hunger, your drive, your desire to be debt free. How badly do you want it? If you truly want to be debt free, you can expect quick and powerful results from the steps in this book.

If you take this seriously, there are big wins just ahead: a side gig that pays your rent, a raise at work that triples your rate of repayment, or a spending plan that frees up an extra $500-$1000 a month.

I want you to go into this with eyes wide open: there is no single solution that will erase your debt overnight. But you also need to know that mainstream advice has it all wrong: you CAN achieve incredible results given a few weeks or months.

Later, we'll figure out exactly how long you'll be in debt, but for now, know that it is your willingness to follow through on these steps that matters most in determining your success.

My Story and Why You Need This Book

Someone's coming towards me.

Was I spotted? What time is it? Half-baked questions race through my groggy mind as I struggle to wake up.

A faint light shines through the synthetic material of my camouflage bivy sack (think of a sleeping bag that works like a tent – it's essentially a waterproof body condom).

I freeze and listen carefully to the outside world.

Tap, tap, tap, tap, tap, tap. Whatever it is, it's getting closer.

I quietly unzip my no-see-um mosquito netting just enough to take a peek. A runner's shoe lands inches from my face...

...and continues onwards out of sight.

I check my phone: it's 5:30am. I've overslept.

Not a wise thing to do when you're sleeping in the woods on public property... illegally.

I roll up my mat, stuff my gear into my lightweight hiker's backpack, and trek towards work in my gym shorts and t-shirt.

Just another day paying off debt.

Four months later...

I'm in a strange house, in a strange bed, alone. And I'm laughing like a madman.

Did I go crazy? Did sleeping in the woods for four months push me over the edge?

No – this laughter (and if I'm being honest, tears of joy) was the result of something all sane people desire and hunger for: freedom. More specifically: financial freedom.

In only four months I'd paid off ALL of my $25,000 in credit card debt, drastically reduced my living expenses, and tested a ton of income earning strategies – some of which paid over half the salary of my full-time job at a tech startup.

And the best part?

None of the hard work or cost-saving measures I'd undertaken actually felt like sacrifice.

Surprisingly, all my efforts – from sleeping in the woods to naming porn flicks for cash (yes, really) – felt like progress towards a better, brighter future. A life where I would be free from the bondage to which I'd grown accustomed over the previous five years. A future where I could travel, start a business, and be open to life's adventures.

And I'd finally achieved it.

So yeah, I was happy.

For a good five minutes, I laughed uncontrollably as my cheek muscles burned from a painfully large smile. I didn't know if the windows were open, or if my neighbors were locking their doors and hiding their children, but I didn't care if I sounded insane.

I was finally free. I was in control of my future. I was ALIVE.

Paying off my debt wasn't easy, but it was worth it. It was good for my health, my wealth, and my future.

As you'll see, my story begins with the stereotypical millennial growing pains: too much spending, too little concern for the health of one's finances, and an ever-growing pile of debt that's shoved under the rug and ignored as much as possible.

Where it differs is how it ends. While many of my friends were dutifully paying their minimum payments and clocking their 9-5, I knew that life wasn't for me. Mainstream advice tells you to put money into savings, make your minimum payments, and stick to it… but that takes forever.

I'm too impatient for that.

Instead, I started experimenting with alternative (some would say stupid) ways of making money and cutting costs. And in the end, I achieved the freedom I craved so desperately – and I did it much faster than anyone thought possible.

Some of the tricks I picked up along the way are crazy – like did you know that in some states you can sell other people's businesses (acting as a broker) without a license?

I had no training and no experience, but $250 in advertising closed a deal and I got a check for five thousand dollars (you'll hear the whole story in Chapter 10).

Or are you aware of the countless jobs you can do to earn money quickly on sites like Amazon's Mechanical Turk, or Upwork, or Fiverr? And don't let "I'm not qualified" or "I don't know how to do that" be an excuse. You can learn new skills for free on Coursera.com or edX.

Even if there's something super specific you need to learn, you can probably find an eBook that'll teach you the step-by-step process.

For example, I accepted a job creating pay-per-click advertising campaigns on Google AdWords and only after getting the job did I bother figuring out how to do it. This might sound like a recipe for disaster, but you'd be surprised how quickly you can learn things from a book or blog post.

A $10 eBook got me a $1,000 paycheck for about 10 hours of work. You call it lucky? I call it "just in time learning." It's a thing. Google it.

My four months paying off debt taught me a lot, and I want to share every shortcut and resource I discovered with you.

But before we get into the good stuff, here are a few things I want to say up front.

You are not alone

When I first began sharing my debt freedom story, I quickly realized that I was not alone – there are a TON of people out there suffering from debt-related anxiety.

In fact, over 66% of the 80 million millennials in the U.S. have one or more sources of long-term debt. And at the time of this publishing, 8 out of 10 Americans have some type of debt.

My point is this: there is a ridiculous amount of debt in this country.

For many of us, it's a pretty stressful thing to deal with. I'll never forget how helpless I felt: worrying about putting food on the table, feeling like I was drowning in interest fees, scared that I was losing control of my future.

No one should have to feel that way. And if you feel at all like that now, I want to do everything I can to help you.

This book is for you if...
- You are in a little debt and want to sprint fast, or
- You are in a lot of debt and want to run the marathon faster

This book is NOT for you if...
- You're looking to get rich overnight
- You want someone else to do the heavy lifting for you
- You are resistant to new ideas and unwilling to try new things

This book is not politically correct, and I'm going to throw some unusual and sometimes downright questionable ways of saving and making money at you. I will never recommend you do anything unethical or illegal.

What you can expect from me

First and foremost, you can expect me to:

1. Tell the truth
2. Only recommend tools and resources I've used and believe in
3. Share practical tips that you can read about in seconds and get results with in minutes

I'm not here to preach to you. I'm here to guide you.

Expect straightforward explanations and easy to follow Action Steps. NO finance-speak, NO get rich quick schemes, NO BS.

This is the book I wish I'd had when I was first getting started. Debt can be isolating and confusing, and as soon as you start searching for ways to make money you'll come across tons of time wasters.

Pyramid schemes, blog posts full of affiliate links trying to make money on your confusion, an endless parade of people whose *only* experience with making money is through selling you a "how to make money" course or book.

This isn't that. Everything I recommend you do, *I've* personally done myself.

How to Use This Book

Anyone can pick up this book and read it – but not everyone will see results.

The difference between the person who uses this book to quickly eliminate their debt and the person who reads this book but fails to make changes is one small thing: *action*.

To get the most out of this book, you must do 2 things:
1. Be open to accepting new ideas.
2. Take action and implement the money strategies into your life.

In this book you'll learn a whole new approach to paying off debt. I encourage you to read it with an open mind. You may be familiar with some of the concepts. You may have an urge to get defensive when I discuss debt as a "problem."

Instead of brushing this off and saying, "That's not me, I'm different" I encourage you to think deeply about it and be honest with yourself.

But you can't just read a book and expect it to get you results. Your results depend on YOU taking action based on the reading.

That's why I made this a step-by-step book. So you can take action while you're reading.

If you do this, I promise you your experience with money will transform, you'll find a new joy in dealing with your finances, and you'll start becoming the true master of your future.

Of course, you can't just read a book and expect it to do the work for you. Your results depend on how much action you take based on the steps and principles in this book.

Let me repeat that: You must take action. If you just read straight through, you'll learn a lot – but nothing will change. That's why this is a "step by step" book with extremely specific instructions.

Some of the steps can be done immediately, while others will take a bit longer. For the longer steps, feel free to continue through the book before you've finished them, but always START an Action Step as soon as you come to it.

It will be tempting to put it off until tomorrow when you "have more time." One of the first things you should know is that time does not matter. "When will I have time for this?" is not a useful question. Here's a better one: "Will I be more or less likely to want to do this tomorrow?"

Don't manage your time, manage your energy and motivation.

If you follow the steps, I promise you your relationship with money and debt will change completely. You will improve your cash flow and start paying off your debt faster. You will also find renewed energy and determination.

Whether you have a little credit card debt, huge student loans, are living paycheck to paycheck at your parent's house, or are making 6-figures while servicing 6-figure debt… it doesn't matter.

This system will give you the foundation and tools you need to take control of your finances. If you follow all the steps, by the end of this book…

- You'll have your money management on autopilot
- You'll know how much to put towards which debt, and exactly when to do it
- You'll be able to make purchases stress-free, without kicking yourself every time you buy something nice (yes – you can be in

debt *and* enjoy your life. In fact, you'll be more likely to succeed if you do.)
- You'll be the master of finding new money-making opportunities, so you can supercharge your race to debt freedom

How to Destroy Your Debt

This book is divided into three parts:

1. The Winner's Mindset
2. Your Money Framework
3. Incredible Profitability

Part 1 will give you the mindsets and psychological strategies that are essential for tackling debt and building wealth through creative, unconventional tactics. You will take steps to jumpstart your momentum and put you on the fast track to financial success.

Part 2 will establish a foundation for straightforward, effortless money management. You will learn how to painlessly track your debt and your money, and you will create a debt elimination plan that leaves no room for doubt about when to pay, what to pay, or how much to pay.

Part 3 will skyrocket your profitability by implementing powerful measures to reduce your expenses and increase your income. You will learn how to negotiate a raise, get more and better job offers, or even find a totally new job.

There are also some, shall we say, less traditional strategies here that can score you some major side income. Not everything will be a good fit for everyone – and that's OK – but I guarantee that if you approach this section with an open mind, you'll find a way to cut months or even years off your debt repayment journey.

Now that you know what's coming your way, it's time to get started. The way you deal with debt and money is about to change forever...

Part I:

The Winner's Mindset

Chapter 1

What Kind of Life Do You Want?

"If you know the enemy and know yourself, you need not fear the result of a hundred battles."
– SUN TZU

I got hooked at an early age.

I was awkward and introverted in college. At first I struggled to make friends, but over time I found that I could increase my status - and get more dates - by dropping cash on expensive clothes and buying drinks at the bar.

This trend continued into my early twenties. After I graduated college on the west coast, I moved to Boston to start a new job – and once again, spending money on nights out on the town proved to be an effective strategy for meeting new people and building a friendship circle from scratch.

By 2014 I was successful and happy – at least that's what you'd think if you met me. Strutting around town in expensive clothes, eating at fancy restaurants, living downtown in my one-bedroom apartment... I was about as yuppie as it gets.

But the good times weren't to last.

During the previous few years, I'd let an insidious force take hold in my financial life. While I was lucky enough to not have student loan debt, I'd been using credit cards to pay for my happy-go-lucky millennial lifestyle.

If a financial adviser had looked at my spending, they'd have been shocked: I spent about 50% of my income on rent, and the remaining 50% was eaten up quickly thanks to expensive dinners and fancy cocktails.

If I was good at anything, it was burning through cash. But I was 25, working at a cool company, and in the prime of my life (or so I thought) – no one was going to tell me how to live, and I never sought money advice from anyone.

And so, the debt kept growing. A round of drinks here, a platter of oysters there... and soon I had a mountain of debt on my shoulders. It was intangible. It was hidden in bits and bytes in computer databases. But it was there.

How bad was it? I didn't even know. I avoided my credit statements like the plague. I knew I was in debt. I knew it was something to deal with at some point. But that was future Charlie's problem. Not something to be concerned with in the present.

To make matters worse, I had delusions of grandeur that would make a psychiatrist cry.

I grew up in a culture of "I can do anything," and I was surrounded by achievers. I was sure I was going to be a rock star entrepreneur, a billionaire businessman.

When I got coins as change for my bills, I'd simply leave them at the counter and walk away with only my light and valuable dollars in my pocket. Quarters, dimes, nickels and pennies... none of it was worth my soon-to-be-Rockefeller time.

I read about successful entrepreneurs getting rich in their twenties and knew that I could do the same.

This sense of being capable of doing anything was reinforced by the people I hung out with. Many of my friends were entrepreneurs or people working the startup grind, and we'd all drunk the "soon-to-be-successful" Kool-Aid.

The rationale went something like this:
- I'm successful and capable of anything, so
- I'm going to be a millionaire before I'm 30, so
- I don't need to worry about my measly debt, it's chump change anyways.

So yes… I was a bit delusional back then.

Don't get me wrong – those ambitious goals are 100% possible. But they have to be earned.

Had I been building a business, with proven customers and a product that they were just itching for… that would have been one thing.

But at the time, I was merely "playing at entrepreneurship." I was a classic wantrepreneur.

I ordered my embossed business cards from Moo.com. I paid for the premium LinkedIn account. I had my suits custom-fitted by a traveling company based in Thailand (and yes, they accepted American Express).

I talked about startup validation techniques and lean customer development, but I rarely put the knowledge into practice.

I only checked my credit card balance a few times during that period… and only after some motivational "self-talk" and a couple glasses of wine.

For me, looking into my financial situation was about as painful as facing my fear of public speaking. I'd break out in cold sweats, my anxiety would soar through the roof, and my hands would shake like early onset Parkinson's.

But one day, everything changed...

"I'm sorry sir, your card's been declined."

A straightforward statement, but it didn't compute in my rich-guy-wannabe brain.

"Sir, do you have another card you want me to use?"

I remember looking up from my apparently worthless credit card to see the concerned face of a Chipotle cashier staring back at me.

I didn't know what to say. I'd already maxed out all my other cards and this one was supposed to last me until my next paycheck – still a couple days away.

I managed to find the words, "Uh, no thanks I actually need to go" and hurried outside.

I'll never forget how ashamed, embarrassed, and afraid I was. I couldn't afford food? The most basic of all purchases? Was I really, truly broke? How did I let things get so bad?

Not being able to afford lunch was the proverbial punch in the face: it felt awful, but it immediately got my full attention. It was a wake-up call that forced me to finally face my situation and come to grips with reality.

That day, I went home and looked up the balance on every credit card I had. The grand total? I was $25,000 in debt.

But wait: it gets worse! The actual debt was bad enough, but a quick look into my accounts revealed that my interest rates were through the roof.

Even though I was paying more than my minimums each month, my high interest fees ate up most of the payments, leaving my balance mostly untouched.

I have always prided myself on being independent, yet here I was utterly dependent on someone else's money.

It was infuriating.

At that moment, I committed myself to becoming debt free... by whatever means necessary.

What's So Bad About Debt?

Before you can conquer your enemy, you need to understand your enemy.

Let's take a few minutes to make sure we're on the same page when we talk about the "D" word.

What I'm about to say may sound extreme or hyperbolic, but trust me - just because our culture accepts debt as a necessary evil doesn't mean that it's harmless or benign.

After all, this is the same culture that got half a generation hooked on smoking. This is the same culture that brought us a *sequel* to Hot Tub Time Machine. The truth is that debt ruins lives every day.

Debt isn't just a loan, or a line of credit: it is a dangerous, potentially lethal financial instrument. And while it can absolutely be used for good (such as getting an education that triples your earning potential), excess debt is nothing but toxic.

Too much debt can destroy you. It can come out of nowhere and explode like an atom bomb, obliterating your savings and ruining your peace and happiness. Or it can cozy up next to you, looking friendly and harmless at first, but slowly increasing the heat until — like a frog in a pot of water — the undetectable changes in temperature arrive at a boiling point, burning you up and searing your future like an ahi tuna steak at a seafood grill.

No matter how excess debt enters your life, the results are always the same: fear, stress, and frustration.

Debt isn't just borrowed money that needs to be repaid. Debt is an agreement to pay the money back *PLUS interest*. The former is straightforward and easy to understand. The latter is the black widow spider whose small size hides its deadly bite.

Burning Dollar Bills

Each of your debts has an interest rate. It's what makes debt a worthy investment for lenders. (If this seems too basic to you, just bear with me for a few of paragraphs. We'll get into the good stuff in a sec.)

The interest rate is a percentage (e.g., 20% a year) that is applied to your balance (the total amount you owe) to determine a fee you must pay the lender. This fee is the price you pay for having the benefit of using someone else's money.

Every time these fees are calculated — automatically, silently — they are quietly added to the total amount you owe, increasing your debt one little (or perhaps not so little) fee at a time. This also means that each *previous* fee contributes to you paying more in *future* fees.

That's compound interest. And you do NOT want it working against you.

For example:

Let's say you owe $10,000 on a credit card with an interest rate of 19%. Your minimum monthly payment is $200, and you always pay the minimum amount due. You never overpay, but you also never miss a payment.

Does this sound crazy? It doesn't to me at first glance. You're making your minimum payments, which sounds like a good thing. Yeah, you've got $10K in debt, but that's not nearly as bad as the size of some of the student loans I hear my friends complaining about.

Here's the kicker:

If you only pay the minimum payment each month on this credit card, you'll be paying this debt off for 100 months. That's over 8 years.

But that's not the worst part. You borrowed $10,000 by spending money on your credit card, but by the time you pay the entire balance back, you'll have paid back $19,795: the $10,000 you owed, plus $9,795 in interest fees.

How is this possible? Your interest rate is compounding, so it builds on itself.

When you deposit $10,000 in a savings account that has a 1% interest rate, you are *earning* compound interest:
- You start with a $10,000 balance
- You earn interest of 1% ($100), so now you have a $10,100 balance

- Later you earn another interest payment of 1%, but this time the interest payment is a little higher ($101) because your balance was a little higher
- So you end up with a balance of $10,201

As you can see, the interest you're getting paid is increasing over time – slowly, but surely.

This is all well and good when compound interest is working *for you*. But with debt, the opposite is true. Your interest COSTS are the lender's interest INCOME.

And this all happens automatically, whether you're aware of it or not.

Hazardous to Your Health

If excess debt only torpedoed your financial health, that would be motivation enough to get rid of it. Unfortunately, its impact on your physical and mental health is equally damaging – if not more so. Here are some more reasons you should want to destroy your debt.

People with large amounts of debt have significantly higher blood pressure levels and report being in worse health in general than people without high debt levels, per one study.

High blood pressure is a serious risk factor for heart disease and stroke (two things you REALLY don't want.) These results were found *despite* the fact that the study participants were between the ages of 24 and 32 – this surprised even the study's author, who said:

"We were...surprised to see these effects in people so young and otherwise healthy...it just goes to show you how salient debt is as a health issue in today's society." – Elizabeth Sweet, Ph.D.

If debt was a prescription drug being advertised on TV, we'd still only be halfway through the "side effects include" fine print at the end. Debt has been linked to depression, stress, anxiety, increased visits to the doctor, and impaired immune system functioning.

And you thought the money part was bad...

The Relationship Killer

There's one other cost of debt that isn't talked about as much, but is important to be aware of, and that's the impact on your relationships. Be it your family, your friends, your spouse or significant other – debt's impact is insidious and destructive – and you might not even be aware of it.

> "Arguments about money [are] by far the top predictor of divorce"
> – Sonya Britt, Kansas State University researcher.

Couples who disagree about financial issues regularly are much more likely to divorce within five years than those who argue about other issues (chores, in-laws, quality time, sex), according to a study.

Have you ever argued with someone about money? It's a terrible thing to experience.

If you're married or in a committed relationship, try to think back to any conflicts you might have been through, or any ongoing tension or frustration that may still exist.

Often, couples have different expectations about what is or is not appropriate when it comes to spending money, or what that money should be spent on.

And if you have or are planning on having kids, consider how debt affects children. Remember how we just talked about money causing stress, anxiety, and a whole host of other psychological effects? You can bet that's not going to be a good influence on your kids.

If there's tension or arguing in the home, what message is that going to send them? Instead of seeing money as a positive thing – a tool to be used for good – your children will see money as a source of conflict, as something that can hurt people.

Whether you're married, in a committed relationship, dating or single, take a few minutes to think about how debt may have affected your relationships (partner, family, friends).

Avoid the Guilt Trap

As you take the first steps toward eliminating your debt, I need to warn you about a trap that's lying in wait for you. In fact, you may have already fallen victim to it. It's called "the Guilt Trap."

The Guilt Trap is when you fall into the vicious cycle of self-blame and guilt due to having too much debt. It's the idea that you are at fault, that you have done something stupid, or something bad – that you are guilty of stupidity or serious mistakes.

The Guilt Trap is dangerous because it puts you in the position of choosing between two inaccurate options:

1) **Shoot-Yourself-In-The-Foot Option:** You are guilty of doing something stupid or naive for getting yourself into debt and should be blamed for your current circumstance, or

2) **Life-Is-Unfair Option:** Someone else is guilty of putting you in this situation and they should be blamed for your debt or money troubles.

In reality, neither of these are likely to be true. For most people, debt is a product of all sorts of things: culture, upbringing, social norms, cost of living, and economic hardship.

From the perspective of paying off your debt, it doesn't matter who or what's to blame for the fact that you're in debt. The only thing that matters is what you do now.

The Guilt Trap is a waste of your time. Don't fall for it.

Instead, you must ditch the idea of guilt altogether.

You have a new word you're going to use: OWNERSHIP.

You OWN this problem. It's your problem. You are responsible for it. You will deal with it.

While guilt is associated with fault and punishment, ownership is associated with responsibility and accountability. Guilt is negative, punitive, harmful. Ownership is positive and constructive.

When you take ownership over your debt problem instead of blaming yourself (or someone else) for it, you start taking responsibility for it. You begin acting as the boss of "Team You" and you will look for solutions and paths forward.

Instead of wallowing in guilt and shame, you start taking action.

If you can adopt an ownership mindset, you will find yourself with a "take charge attitude" and will already be on your way to developing a powerful source of motivation, positive energy, and determination.

This is a critical component in our process, so before you move on to the next chapter, make a conscious decision that you will not blame yourself (or anyone else) for your debt problem. You will not feel guilty about your present circumstance.

Instead, you will take ownership of it.

Meet Matt

With a burning desire for financial independence, I decided to start a food truck business.

I was seeing food truck success stories all over the place, and the idea of being in control of my own destiny was irresistible. I raised $100,000 to pay for the truck and startup costs, then got to work on building a rock star business.

Unfortunately, things went wrong right from the start.

My franchise partner, who'd promised tons of support to get me up and running, was suddenly "unavailable." Then after paying for the truck and equipment, I discovered the vendor had done a shoddy job and the truck was unreliable.

To make matters worse, my co-founder – who I depended on to help with sales – turned out to be a complete flake and rarely showed up for work.

I pushed forward with dreams of grandeur, but as the months passed by, it became clear things weren't going to work out. Sales were slow, and I was racking up debt quickly on my credit cards to pay for basic expenses.

Have you ever seen Arrested Development? "I've made a terrible mistake."

This was one of the worst times of my life. I would wake up depressed and go to work with an enormous weight on my back. I had no idea how I was going to salvage the situation.

After a few more months of poor sales, I decided to sell the truck. I had to sell at a huge loss, but I was determined to repay my investors.

After the dust settled I walked away with $20,000 of credit card debt and a depleted savings account. I had to move back in with my parents since I couldn't afford an apartment, and I started taking online classes to try to reboot my career.

It was an incredibly stressful time. I felt like a failure, and since I'd borrowed money from family and friends, my failure felt very public.

It took a while, but eventually I found a good job and paid off my debt. In fact, now that I'm debt-free and making good money, I recently decided to invest in a rental property and continue working towards my goal of having passive income and financial freedom.

Here's my advice:

First and foremost, if you've made mistakes and accumulated a lot of debt, don't let that be an excuse to give up on your financial goals. Sure, having thousands (or hundreds of thousands) of dollars of debt sucks, but it's not the end of the world. Get some perspective and remember that things could be worse.

And second, if you're paying someone else 18% interest because you have a shit-ton of credit card debt, then you need to make it a priority! By carrying a balance, you're paying for the CEO of American Express to get a 10 million dollar bonus. Stop it!

- Matt. C

ACTION STEP 1: Accept the Debt Challenge

Let me ask you a basic, but very important question: *Do you have a debt problem?*

Be brutally honest with yourself. It's natural to get a little defensive – and that's OK. I was in complete denial about my problem with debt until a Chipotle burrito woke me up to the truth.

But before you brush this aside or minimize the impact of debt in your life, take a minute to answer the following questions:

- Has your credit card ever been declined due to insufficient funds?
- Have you ever been ashamed or embarrassed about your debt?
- Are any of your credit cards maxed out?
- Are you only making the minimum payments on your debt?
- Have you ever avoided checking your bank account, card statement, or opening mail from a lender?
- Does your debt cause stress, worry, or create tension for you?
- Have you ever borrowed money to pay off other debts?

Similar to diagnosing a disease, if you have one or more of the above symptoms you may have a debt problem. Really take some time to think about these questions.

Try to remember specific experiences from your life. I know you may be anxious to get on with the book and into the meat of the solution to your debt, but it's critical that you have a clear and accurate understanding of how debt affects you before we go any further.

When it comes to money and debt, most people are closed off to new ideas. They think, "This is basic stuff. I already know how to manage my money. I might have a little debt right now, but that'll change. It's just a matter of time."

I get it. Money is a sensitive topic. Most people believe they are quite capable of managing their money, and by opening themselves up to new ideas – especially about debt – they essentially question that ability. It's a gut punch to the ego.

But let me ask you a question…

How well has your current approach to money served you up to this point?

If you're not having the success with money you want, and if you're not improving your cash flow, then your ideas are probably holding you back.

Whether you call your debt a burden, a challenge, a nuisance, or a problem – it's important to acknowledge that it's there. You need to recognize it and admit that it affects you in real, tangible ways.

Did you answer yes to any of the questions?

If so, you very likely have a debt problem. The more yeses, the more serious the problem. If you are in debt but answered "no" to all of the above, then the good news is that you're likely in a situation where your debt is something you can handle. The bad news is (of course) – you're still in debt.

Either way, you're about to follow a series of steps that will change all that.

So right now, it's time to make a decision and complete your first Action Step.

Do you accept The Debt Challenge?

If you answer "yes," then for the rest of this book, you are committing to me, and yourself, that you will take this matter seriously and put forth extra effort to create real change in your life.

If you answer "no," then this is where we part ways.

Yes --> Go to the next page.

No --> Go back to your old life.

...still with me?

Great! Onwards and upwards.

Chapter 2

Light the Fire: Bullet-Proof Resilience and Limitless Motivation

"It's not what you do, but why you do it."
— SIMON SINEK

I was fat.

It was 2014 and I was living in Boston, where I was currently in my apartment looking into a mirror and squeezing a flabby chunk of flesh from my gut.

Over the course of months and months of late nights out drinking with friends, coming back home with the drunchies (drunk munchies, for the uninitiated) to eat junk food, and not making enough time for exercise, I'd managed to gain some pure, white, blubber.

I was disgusted by it.

I'd always taken pride in my discipline and dedication towards my goals. But somehow, though I valued physical fitness, I'd let myself slide.

How had I let things get this far? Once upon a time I was lean, fit, and muscular... whatever happened to that guy?

The last time I'd been so chunky was when I was a kid.

I can still remember huffing and puffing as I tried to keep up with the other kids while running around the football field in what felt like endless circles. Red in the face, sucking in air as fast as I could, the only thing that kept me going was the fear (probably justified) that the other kids would laugh at me if I gave up.

That all changed when I got to high school and discovered girls.

Teenage Charlie, who was no fool, quickly realized that girls liked guys who were popular, physically attractive, and funny. I had no idea how to be popular or funny, but I saw fit guys working out at the school gym all the time. Surely, lifting weights must be the ticket to an attractive body. So, I started working out.

I'll be honest: if I hadn't cared about wanting to be attractive to girls, I wouldn't have started exercising. Without the desire to attract the opposite sex, I probably would've continued burning through my youth playing video games in dark basements and eating carbo-licious pizza any chance I got.

But instead I got in shape.

Not because it was fun – it was miserable (at first). Not because it was easy – it was hard. I got in shape for exactly one reason: it would get me closer to my goal of a date with a girl.

Now back to 2014 and that chunky white guy in the mirror.

I remember looking back on my childhood and reflecting on how motivated I became as soon as girls entered the picture.

It had changed everything: I paid more attention to how I looked, how I talked, the pitch of my voice, even the way I smelled. It affected damn near every decision I made throughout my daily life.

And then it clicked: back then, I had found a powerful motivator.

In the months following my realization by the mirror, I would go through a similar process of losing weight and getting fit, just as I'd done all those years before. But this time, I leveraged my motivator consciously and deliberately.

I knew that one of my weaknesses was coming home late at night after a long day at the office, and then drinking too much wine while I gobbled up too much food.

I'd typically sit down on the couch with a plate of relatively healthy food. So far so good. Then, after a glass or two of wine, I'd get more and more tempted by the less health-friendly items in the fridge. My go-to was chips and hummus.

Harmless in small quantities, but add stress and fatigue and that seemingly healthy snack turns into a calorie-laden food coma.

To combat this, I needed a way to short-circuit the process.

My solution?

I put a Victoria's Secret magazine in the fridge.

Some things never change.

Every time I opened the refrigerator door, there she was. Some beautiful, bikini-clad model whose name I don't remember, staring at me, judging me as I pulled food out of the fridge.

Every time I was tempted to overindulge, there it was: a good reason NOT to.

A reminder of something I cared about more than an extra helping.

I'd still get home from work stressed out and tired, but when I went to reach into the fridge I'd get an instant dose of motivation. It worked so well that often, I'd close the refrigerator door and do a half hour workout before eating anything.

Within a few weeks, I'd lost a sizable chunk of that original fistful of blubber. Within months, I began showing more muscle definition.

But the progress didn't stop there.

It was now mid-2014, and I was seriously in debt.

Remembering my successful experiment losing weight, I decided to try to apply something similar to my debt problem.

Creating my new motivator was simple. I used a pen, paper, fifteen minutes and a little honest thinking. At the end of that fifteen minutes, I wrote down a single sentence:

Beautiful women want to have sex with attractive men who don't have debt.

Beneath that I wrote my debt number (the sum of all my debt balances). Then I folded the paper in half and tucked it in my wallet.

I actually had an even bigger reason to want to get out of debt – more on that in just a minute.

But this was a great, instant reminder of my priorities.

Moving forward, anytime I looked into my wallet I would see that little slip of paper. And should I be tempted to do something stupid with my money – like buy a round of expensive drinks for people at the bar – I would first be forced to think about how it would affect my future relationship prospects.

The important thing about my motivator in both of these cases was that it didn't *force* me to sacrifice, it didn't force me to stop doing the thing I wanted to do; instead, it gently reminded me to think about my current actions in the context of my larger goal. Because of that, it felt like empowerment instead of sacrifice.

And by having the reminder at the precise moment that I was considering straying from my goal, I was given the chance to make a more conscious and aware decision.

This is what made it so effective.

I know my motivator may seem silly, or vain, or shallow to some people... but it didn't harm anyone, *and it worked*. (By the way, to any ladies out there who are asking themselves, "Are guys really that simple?" I offer you the following: No comment.)

Meet Andrew

My life in the US started with debt.

As a Canadian, I had to take out personal loans from friends and family, and regular loans from a bank and the government, to pay the high tuition costs of going to university in Boston. It wasn't the best timing. It was 2008 and I watched the Canadian dollar weaken while my tuition bills continued to grow each year.

I quickly became overwhelmed with each semester's expenses, and I started to doubt whether I'd be able to borrow enough money to graduate.

I made the unfortunate decision to ignore the problem. I took on the mentality that I might as well have fun and not let money slow down my social life, since I would surely either drown financially or I'd make enough money that a few thousand in credit card debt wouldn't really matter.

I barely managed to graduate, with the total bill coming to $156,690 in student loans and $7,500 in credit card debt.

Now that I was out of college, I was ready to discover the business side of the world through sales. Though I struggled to find my stride at first, I set aggressive goals and forged my own path forward. I made an effort to find great mentors and I relentlessly chased companies and job opportunities I was passionate about, which made interviewing and networking easier.

I eventually found a job I was excited about that paid well, and by focusing on personal and career development, I quickly improved my skills and was able to double my salary in 18 months.

Now that I had a stable job, I became determined to prove those who doubted me wrong. I felt there was a consensus among my friends back home that I would be in debt forever, and this inspired me to commit to getting out of debt fast.

There were two big things that had a profound impact on my finances. The first was finding a motivator to get me excited about paying off debt. For me, this was the prospect of owning property and putting my money to work for me. To do this, I'd have to pay off my debt.

The second thing was I decided to give 20% of my net income to charity. This principle had been the cornerstone of my life until midway through college, and resuming this focus on contribution gave my financial life new meaning and purpose.

My advice:

I highly recommend finding ways to motivate yourself and find meaning in what you do. It's what has helped me pay off $17,862 of debt over the past few years and is keeping me on track to pay much more now that I've increased my income.

- Andrew H.

Why do YOU want to be debt free?

"It's not *what* you do, but *why* you do it," said Simon Sinek in one of the most viewed TED Talks of all time.

From Apple, to Martin Luther King, to the Wright Brothers, Sinek goes into detail showing how it was the "why" that mattered in their success, more than the "what."

There are a lot of psychology, biology, and marketing concepts that go into the power of why, but right now I want to talk about how this relates to debt.

Think about it for a moment – what's wrong with being in debt? Millions of other Americans are in debt, after all. You're just one in a sea of countless others, and what's wrong with that?

I asked this question at one of my Boston Debt Destroyers meetings not long ago and got the following answers:

- I don't want to worry about money anymore
- I want to be able to start saving money to buy a house
- I want to be free to make my own choices in life

Obviously, it's a given that debt isn't a great thing to have: you don't want to owe people money.

Here's the thing, though: *that's not enough.*

I've learned that if you're going to fight debt head-on, to take it seriously and start trying new and creative ways to get out of debt, you're going to need more than a vague notion for why you're doing this.

There are many reasons to get out of debt, just like there are all sorts of reasons to lose weight. But not all reasons are created equal. Some are much more powerful than others.

The goal of this exercise is simple.

I want to you to find your #1 reason for why you want to be debt free. This "why" is your Debt Freedom Purpose.

Your DFP is a must-have resource, like when a boxer in the ring takes his corner and is given a quick pep talk by his coach. That tough, scrappy little coach is your DFP. When debt roughs you up a bit, just take a step back, regroup with your DFP, and come back into the ring swinging.

Everyone's debt freedom purpose is a little different.

You might want to be debt free so you can travel the world and have exciting new adventures. Or maybe you want to eliminate debt to be better positioned to start a family or buy a house. Whatever your reason, it must be something that you really really want.

Here are the key characteristics of a good DFP:

1. You REALLY want it, and
2. You can't achieve it if you stay in debt

And for an extra kick in the butt, find something that matters so much that *not achieving it would make you disappointed in yourself*. I know this sounds extreme, but trust me, it'll help you.

ACTION STEP 2: Find Your Debt Freedom Purpose

1. Grab a piece of paper and write down all your big life goals and aspirations.

Does this sound cheesy? Do it anyway! What you want to do with your life is important. If you're struggling with this, consider the following questions:

Who do you admire? Why?

Where do you see yourself in 5 years?

What does your perfect day look like? (Get specific! How would you want to wake up in the morning? What would you do throughout the day? What's the last thing you'd do before going to bed?)

What makes you happy?

What do you want to do before you die?

Some of the more common goals I've heard include starting a family, buying a house, taking a dream vacation, and changing careers.

Try to write as many goals and aspirations down as possible. This is not the time to censure yourself, and don't hold anything back because it's "too unrealistic." Now is the time to dream big and unleash all the possibilities for your future.

Go old-school on this: write your goals/aspirations on an actual piece of paper to make it feel more real and tangible. Trust me, it makes a difference.

2. Put a star next to any of the goals or aspirations that you've thought about for a while (say, more than a year).

We do this to ensure your DFP will matter to you for the entire time you're in debt. While some goals fade with time, goals that you've had for more than a year are more likely to matter to you for another year or longer.

If you have a burning, insatiable desire to achieve something and it only just came into your life recently, don't toss it out – it's still valid, but see if it passes the next test.

3. Cross out any of your goals or aspirations that would be easy for you to do while you're still in debt.

It's time to put your goals on the chopping block. Now is when you get tough and cross out anything that would be too easy to accomplish from your current state of indebtedness.

Winning a pie eating contest by cramming twelve apple pies down your gullet might satisfy your bucket list (though... really?), but you could probably pull this off while still in debt. Nix it and move on.

4. Choose your Debt Freedom Purpose.

At this point you should be left with goals that you REALLY want to achieve, and only ones you can't accomplish easily while in debt.

Review your options and pick the most compelling one. Remember, this is now your purpose for wanting to be debt free. This needs to inspire you, motivate you, energize you. If the goals you're considering don't ignite just a little bit of fire in your heart, then go back to square one and start over.

Take my DFP for example: I wanted to be debt free so I could start a business.

Side note: My original motivator was "being attractive to women", but after some deep reflection, I picked "starting a business" and felt an even greater pull towards freedom.

Starting a business was something I'd thought about for years – on some level, I was always thinking about it. I'd tried to start businesses in the past, but with money being tight, they'd inevitably fizzle out as I lost momentum and went back to focusing on my career.

But despite this, I always self-identified as an entrepreneur. To me, creating a business was part of my life's great work – something that I needed to do. Not doing this would mean failure, and I would be devastated if I never at least gave it a fair shot.

With this purpose in mind, my struggle against debt became more meaningful, and I found that I was better equipped to push through the hard stuff to get closer to finally paying off that last bill.

5. Make your DFP visible.

Now that you have a reason why you want to be debt free, it's important to keep it front and center so you never forget it.

I wrote my DFP on a piece of paper and tucked it into my wallet. Anytime I reached into my wallet for my credit card I'd have an "Oh yeah!" moment where I saw my reason for battling debt and I'd immediately feel a boost of willpower and energy.

A friend of mine taped his purpose on the wall above his bed. The first thing he saw every morning was a reason to get out of bed and go conquer debt. Another debtor told me he put his DFP on the wall of his cubicle at work.

Whether it's a sticky note on the fridge or a reminder in Google Calendar, just make sure you're reminded on a regular basis. The human brain is great at conveniently forgetting things related to a sore subject (like your finances), and this is one resource you cannot afford to lose track of.

Now that you have an awesome reason to get free of your debt, let's start building some serious debt-destroying momentum.

Chapter 3

System Reset: Escaping Paralysis and Igniting Rocket Fuel

"Go as far as you can see, when you get there, you'll be able to see farther."
— J.P. MORGAN

No booze. No masturbation.

I'd signed up for a 30-day commitment. It was mid 2014, when I was still in debt and spending way too much money going out to drink with friends (though unbeknownst to me, my race to financial freedom was just ahead).

One day I happened across a blog update from Tim Ferriss, the author of "The Four Hour Work Week," talking about the concept of NOBNOM.

NOBNOM stands for NO Booze, NO Masturbation.

Tim asked his readers to try it for one month and see what happened. It was an exercise in discipline and willpower.

I love challenges, and I'm a huge fan of Tim's work, so I decided to go for it.

I emptied out half-drunk bottles of wine and tossed some unopened beers in the trash. Thirty days wasn't a particularly long time, but it was long enough that I didn't want any temptation around.

A month later I was feeling healthier and stronger than ever (and my wallet appreciated life without alcohol too). It wasn't all smooth sailing: throughout the month I'd had a few moments where I had to tell myself, "It's just 30 days, you can do this." But the truth is, while it wasn't a cakewalk, it wasn't nearly as hard as I thought it would be.

And here's where the magic kicks in: by the time the thirty days were up, I felt capable of more.

One month was all it took to prove to myself that I could do it for longer. And so, I did. I continued to the next month, and the next, and the next. If the challenge had been to give up drinking for a year, or six months, or even just a couple months, I never would have considered it.

But 30 days? Anyone can do something for that long. That's nothing.

What's more, after achieving my goal of completing this weird, bizarre NOBNOM thing, *I felt powerful*. It wasn't just that I knew I could do another thirty days if I wanted to – I suddenly felt more capable, more in control. I felt empowered to conquer even greater challenges.

OK, I know talking about masturbation in a book about debt is weird... even as I write this I'm considering deleting it, but there's a reason I include this odd little story here.

I want to illustrate two key points which I'll explain further: the power of the *quick win*, and the concept of *progressive escalation*.

They're related but distinct concepts that I want you to understand so you can use them in your life to not only get out of debt faster, but also anytime you're facing a big ugly challenge that you're struggling with.

The Power of the Quick Win

When I finished the 30 day NOBNOM month, I not only succeeded in breaking my habit of drinking too much, I also proved to myself that I was capable of creating positive change in my life. Don't underestimate how important that is.

When you do something outside of your comfort zone, or something that is a little more challenging than you're used to, it raises an internal fear: *What if I'm not good enough? What if I fail?*

This type of fear can stop you in your tracks. It can keep you from pushing forward and fighting to achieve more.

No one wants to fail. Millions of years of evolution have biologically hardwired our brains to avoid failure at all costs. Thirty thousand years ago, failure to bring home food from the hunt could mean you and your family starve. Failure to observe social norms and traditions could lead to being ostracized and left out in the cold to fend for yourself.

I don't want to fail, and neither do you – which is exactly why getting a quick win is so important.

When you achieve a positive result fast, it does two things:

1. It proves to yourself that you are capable of changing your life and the world, and
2. It breaks any fear and avoidance patterns that may be lurking in your subconscious mind

This is powerful stuff.

With life moving so fast, new technologies being unleashed upon the world, and the internet shoving news, gossip and advertisements in our faces 24/7, it's easy to feel small, unimportant, and incapable of creating meaningful change... even in our own lives.

But that's a lie.

I want you to feel the power of a quick win ASAP – but before you decide what your personal Quick Win challenge will be, I want to introduce some concepts that will be absolutely critical to your success.

The Concept of Progressive Escalation

I was extremely shy when I first got to college. I felt awkward around other people, and I dreaded going to parties.

It was even tougher because many of my friends were charismatic socialites who were always throwing parties and getting our circle of friends invited to off-campus gatherings.

I was a nervous wreck for a solid six months.

But then during a psychology lecture, I discovered a concept that would transform the way I viewed behavior change. A tool that I would use to slowly but surely go from avoiding strangers like the plague to being comfortable talking to people I'd just met (as you can imagine, this also gave a huge boost to my confidence and sense of self-worth).

Here's what I did to overcome my challenge with social interaction:

To start, I wrote down on paper all the different common activities related to socializing that I could think of: talking with someone, going to a party, asking someone the time, asking a girl out on a date, etc.

I then weighed the difficulty of each activity based on my own personal experience and sorted these activities into categories: "easy", "challenging", and "hard."

Finally, I gave myself daily homework assignments, starting with only the easy activities.

Over the following weeks, I would start each day by selecting a social homework assignment. At some point during the day I would work up the courage to complete the activity.

I quickly found that the longer I waited to do the assignment, the harder it became, and there were some days where I built the task up so much in my head that it overwhelmed me and I would chicken out. Soon I learned to tackle my homework assignments first thing in the morning to make sure they got done.

Even the tasks that I thought would be easy were often more difficult than I'd expected, but as the days passed, I got used to them.

A week or two into the experiment, I realized the easy tasks had become too easy and that I was ready to ramp it up a bit. So I started pulling from the "challenging" category. Making constant eye contact with strangers on the street, whistling to myself in public...

Just like before, it started off more difficult than I'd anticipated, but I kept at it – and just like with the "easy" tasks, over a few weeks things became easier.

Finally, I was ready for the hard tasks. I introduced a new hard task once a week. It began with singing in public and progressed to asking a girl out on a date. I'd always hated singing in public; my hands would start shaking and I'd sweat profusely before I even started to sing...

Honestly, it was painful at first. But just like before, I got used to it.

There's a powerful force that comes into play when you start with a small task and gradually progress to increasingly more challenging ones. From a few small wins in the beginning, you build psychological momentum until you've got a snowball of destruction — and you can harness it to get greater and greater results over time.

Take a second to think about a task you've been avoiding, something that you don't want to do.

What is it? Why are you avoiding it? Is there something challenging about it? Is there an "unknown" involved that you don't know how to handle?

If you could take this task and break it into smaller steps, little chunks of effort that add up to the end result, how would you do it?

You can use quick wins and progressive escalation in your battle against debt, or to achieve any challenging goal in life.

You get a quick win — which adds value to your life while also building momentum — and then you begin taking on increasingly more difficult challenges along the path towards an important goal.

As you read on, you'll see that the steps in this book are laid out in a progressive escalation.

Your first Action Step was something you could do right away without a ton of effort, but by the end of this book you'll be trying new things you'd never have considered when you first started.

Some of the tactics in this book may seem a little unusual — even a little crazy. So if at any point you find yourself facing a task too difficult or challenging, consider breaking it down into a progressive escalation.

You can do this by taking the big task and breaking it out into discrete, bite-sized steps that you can tackle one at a time, starting with the easy ones first.

Another option is to simply give yourself a specific deadline for the challenge like we're about to do with a quick win. Whatever challenge you're struggling with, just set a finite period of time that you're going to do it for, and then get started. It's easier to commit to a $300 reduction in your budget for 30 days, then it is to carve out $300 permanently.

And after 30 days (or whatever time increment you choose), you'll have either A) adjusted to the change and will be able to keep going for another 30 days, or B) you'll have just barely made it (or perhaps fallen off the wagon entirely).

If that happens, don't freak out or beat yourself up. Just take a break, reset, and then break the challenge down into smaller bite-sized tasks you know you'll be able to chow down on.

REMEMBER: The power of the quick win and of progressive escalation is in how they affect your behavior. You'll get a boost of motivation and energy from the quick win, and progressive escalation will channel that motivation and energy into a ladder of bite sized steps flowing towards the end goal.

Take Action Every Day

I want you to take action: Every. Damn. Day.

Taking action every day is important, because it creates a sense of momentum in your life. It makes it impossible to feel like you're stagnating.

Instead, you'll have a sense of progress. A sense that you're moving forward and getting closer to achieving your goals. And you will be. But it's important that you feel it. And taking action every day will make you feel it.

> *"Motivation is often the result of action, not the cause of it."*
> – James Clear

Think of it as Newton's First Law applied to your motivation. Objects in motion tend to stay in motion. Motivation works the same way. It's hard to get started, but once you have, it's a lot easier to keep moving forward. (Credit to James Clear for the comparison.)

Taking action every day is a bigger challenge than you might think. When it comes to getting out of debt, much of the day-to-day work isn't that exciting – but hear me out, because there's an easy way to do this (as opposed to the hard way, which is about as fun as eating dry, uncooked oatmeal).

While I am going to push you to take action every day, notice that I didn't say anything about *how much time* you need to spend on this every day. I didn't say you need to commit an hour, or your evenings to this. I'm only asking you to do *something*.

You just need to "show up."

Some days you'll feel energetic, motivated, and have some free time that you can throw into looking for new ways to make money, or put into a side gig you already have. Other days, you won't. That's OK. Just do something.

You'll feel better about your goal and you'll keep the momentum going, which will make it easier to keep taking action and to make more progress the next day, and the next day, etc.

Take this book for example.

My current goal for this book is 100 pages. For someone who's not used to writing, that's a lot of writing.

But I don't have to write all those 100 pages at once. Like we discussed in the concept of progressive escalation, I've broken down this goal into discrete, smaller steps.

Actually, because I *really* need baby steps to keep my momentum going, my to-do list for the day starts with: "Write 1 page of book."

That's it.

After I do that one page, I usually feel better and remember that I've written a handful of pages already, and I just need to keep going, one page at a time. I don't even want to *think* about the 100 pages I need to finish, but by taking it one page at a time I know I can get through this.

Some days I write one page, some days fifteen, but I always write a little. I never let the momentum stop, and you shouldn't either.

Do something productive towards paying off debt every day – even if it's only five minutes of your time.

One trick to do this (which was invented by Jerry Seinfeld – yes, that Seinfeld) is to keep a calendar visible with X's through each day that you make progress on your goal. After a few days, you'll want to keep the chain going. You could also keep a debt journal, or a spreadsheet where you write down what you did each day.

Having a visible representation of your progress will fan the motivational flames.

Willpower is a Limited Resource

I want to make sure you are aware *just how limited* your willpower is on a day-to-day basis.

Now, I'm not saying you don't have any willpower; you do. The very act of buying this book and facing your debt took some willpower, so you absolutely do have willpower at your disposal.

But willpower is a finite, limited resource.

Every day you wake up with a full battery. Your willpower is at maximum capacity and you're good to go. But as you face decisions, obstacles, confusion, and stress throughout the day, your battery depletes – getting reduced by each instance of having to do something you don't naturally enjoy or want to do.

By the end of the day, you may find yourself completely drained, with no willpower left to say "No" to Netflix, Reddit, or other guilty pleasures.

This sounds negative, but knowing that your willpower is limited is actually liberating.

Information is power, and with this knowledge you can leverage your willpower to get better results in paying off your debt.

In your journey to become debt free, you'll likely come across websites, bloggers, friends and well-intentioned acquaintances who share advice like: "no more lattes!" and "collect coupons to save money." You may have already heard this type of rhetoric.

It seems that everyone from the person at the bus stop to your best friend's mother has something to say about saving money, and most of the time the advice involves cutting back on everything, including the little things.

Haircuts, getting lunch out, lattes and cappuccinos, it's easy to point the finger and blame all these little expenses as the sneaky culprits responsible for a lack of savings or a hefty credit card bill. But in fact, these things are probably NOT the reason you are in debt.

Yes, they all play their part: every expense takes away money that could be used to accelerate your path to debt freedom. BUT, the top 20% of your most expensive bills are probably responsible for 80% of your spent money.

This is the 80/20 rule – aka the Pareto Principle – applied to your money.

Here's how it works: Pareto, an economist, found that in many aspects of life, roughly 80% of the results came from just 20% of the causes.

And this is almost certainly true for your debt.

I bet your rent or mortgage is one of your biggest expenses each month. Food, groceries, and dining out probably follow. And then it's either health and medical expenses or some other category like fun and entertainment. Whatever your top 3 biggest expenses are, I can pretty much guarantee they eclipse your bottom 3 expenses.

What does this have to do with limited willpower?

Simply this: you can't focus on reducing ALL your expenses. You don't have enough willpower to cut costs on all fronts at once.

Say you were to eliminate lattes, lunch out with friends, the gym, yoga, renting movies, your TV and internet bundle, and your cell phone plan. If you cut all that out – how would you feel?

Maybe OK for a week, maybe even OK for a month, but indefinitely? You probably wouldn't feel great. You'd probably feel like a "money monk," sacrificing everything at the altar of extreme frugality.

There are two things you should take away from this:

1. Focus your willpower on the important things (like reducing your biggest expenses)

2. Tackle the biggest challenges when you have the most willpower

As you continue down the path of reducing your costs and increasing your income, you may decide to cut some conveniences or luxury expenses that you enjoy and will want to have back later on. This is great, and I applaud your efforts. But I encourage you to focus on the big expenses first.

If you can reduce your housing cost by 10%, I bet you'll save as much (or more) money than if you cut back on lattes for a year, and it'll cost you FAR less willpower, because you only have to do it once. With lattes, you'll have to silence your craving daily.

If you are following the Action Steps in order, you should already have some positive momentum going for you – making it easier to tackle each new challenge you face. But for really big challenges, or tasks that are way outside of your comfort zone, try to confront these when you're feeling fresh in the morning, and not after a long day at the office.

Celebrate Small Wins Along the Way

Ok, just two more concepts to cover before your Quick Win – I promise.

You have a long journey ahead of you. Debt doesn't vanish overnight, it requires sustained, consistent effort over time.

That's not a sexy answer for how to deal with debt, I know, but it's the truth. Some of the methods in this book can dramatically accelerate your progress, but no matter what, the debt isn't going away tomorrow.

Which is why it's important to enjoy your progress along the way.

Motivation fluctuates naturally over time. You'll have up days, down days, and everything in between. How are you feeling now? Motivated? I hope so! But how will you feel in a month from now? I don't know, and honestly, you probably don't know either.

To keep your motivation consistently strong, celebrate small wins along the way.

Here are some "small wins" you might celebrate:

- Getting a quick win under your belt
- Figuring out how much total debt you have
- Figuring out how much money you spend in a typical month
- Creating a spending plan
- Creating a plan to pay off debt
- Paying off your first debt
- Reducing your expenses by $300 each month
- Making your first $100 through a side job

These are just ideas to get you thinking, you can come up with your own.

PRO TIP: Having a high-motivation day? Ride the motivation wave and set up systems that make your life easier. That way, when you're having a low-motivation day, you'll have fewer tasks that require your reduced willpower. For example, put your workout clothes by your bed the night before so it's easier to get up and go the next morning. Or put your debt tracker (we'll create this soon) on your phone so it's front and center.

Celebrate your small wins by indulging in something you enjoy.

This isn't an excuse to overspend or cheat on your budget, but it's OK to spend a little money here and there if it makes you happy and doesn't set you back much. (BTW – it's easier to celebrate small wins when you have a "fun budget" with money dedicated to spending on things like this.)

Guilty pleasures make for great small win celebrations. For example:

- Treat yourself to a glass of wine (or whatever adult beverage you prefer)
- Have a special dessert after dinner
- Go out for dinner
- Rent a movie
- Take a day off from self-imposed work / self-improvement

Consider Having a Kickoff Party

Here's one last tool to add to your paralysis-bustin'-momentum-ignitin' toolkit: having a kickoff party.

When a project manager initiates a new project, they often hold a "project kickoff" meeting involving core team members. It's a way to get everyone who is involved in the project on the same page, while having the added benefit of drawing a clear line in the sand that says "the project has officially begun."

When I first started down the road of paying off debt and exploring extreme tactics to get quick results, I knew I needed a clean "start" – a date that represented the beginning of my work which I could look back on and remember as the starting line. So I had a kickoff party.

I invited a bunch of friends over, asked them to bring food and drinks, and I hosted a party night of games and music. It was fun! My kickoff party was a bit unique, in that I was soon to move out of my apartment and into the woods, so party attendees had the opportunity to win my furniture, my bed, and all the possessions I didn't want to keep, as prizes for winning games.

While giving my stuff away was fun (and allowed me to move out of my apartment quickly), I would recommend you keep your possessions for now and instead open yourself up to the idea of selling some of them later on for cash (we'll talk about this more in Chapter 10).

The kickoff party is still a great idea though.

Your kickoff party could be a get together with friends, a movie night, a game night, or something entirely different. The point is to have an event that marks the starting point of your new (or renewed) focus to become debt free.

You can have a kickoff party all by yourself – maybe you splurge one last time on a guilty pleasure – or it could be with close friends who you want to know about your goal of achieving debt freedom.

Having a kickoff party like this is just an idea, not a requirement of course, but it could be a good way to turn over a new leaf.

ACTION STEP 3: Get a Quick Win

Let's get a quick win under your belt. It doesn't even have to be directly related to your debt – it just needs to be something that will make your life a little bit better.

1. Write down a list of potential challenges.

Jot down a list of things you could do that meet the following criteria:

A) It's an obvious "good thing" – it's good or beneficial for you, and

B) The challenge is just outside your comfort zone

The challenge level should be like the water temperature when you jump in the shower: you want to find that happy medium. This doesn't quite make sense if you're a weirdo who likes freezing cold (like me) or scalding hot showers, but you get the point.

Too difficult, and you'll get stressed and discouraged - you'll burn out. Too easy, and it won't be exciting enough for you to rise to the challenge.

Aim to work just a bit harder than feels comfortable: there's a reason this is called a challenge.

Here are some ideas to consider:

- Give up an expense you enjoy for one week (e.g., drinking or going out for dinner).
- Wake up 30 minutes earlier every day for one week to give yourself time for something healthy. Read an article, get some quick exercise in, or get a jump start on your work for the day.
- Track your spending for one week on a piece of paper (or note on your phone) so you can get an idea of where your money is going.

PRO TIP: Multiply that number by 4 to estimate your monthly spending.

2. Choose your challenge.

Choose wisely. Remember, this needs to be a win! Failure will only deter you from taking on bigger challenges.

Don't make it too easy – it needs to feel like a real win – but don't overstretch. If you're having trouble figuring out how big of a bite to take, then aim smaller for this one. You can take a bigger bite next time.

Remember that the REAL win is following through. Actually doing 10 push-ups every morning is far better than planning to do 100 every day, then burning out in less than a week.

If there's one thing on your list that sounds more fun than the others, do that one. You'll be more motivated to conquer it.

Lastly, trust your gut on this one. Try to find a challenge that you know is inherently good for you. It's easier to push yourself harder when you know it's in your best interest.

3. Choose the duration of the challenge.

Whatever challenge you take on, it must be for a finite period of time.

Here's an example of a bad quick win challenge:

> *"I'm going to stop going out to dinner for as long as I can."*

Here's how we could make that challenge better:

"I'm going to make dinner at home each night for one week instead of going out."

I recommend setting a minimum of a 1 week challenge and a maximum of 4 weeks.

Challenges shorter than a week are often too easy. On the flip side, this is about building momentum quickly – so keep it inside of a month.

Have you ever created a to-do list that got so long you were too intimidated to even start it? The same can happen with your quick win goal. Consider yourself warned.

4. Choose a start date.

This is important. If you don't choose a start date, it's not going to happen. I can't tell you how many times I've written out a list of ambitious goals only to never even attempt them. Writing down goals and challenges is the easy part. The hard part lies in the doing.

Pick your date and set a calendar reminder. Do whatever you need to do to make it abundantly clear to yourself that you're starting the challenge on X date. The calendar app on your phone is a great option since you can set it to automatically give you a pop-up notification. Don't leave any room for the excuse of "I forgot."

That spells death for your quick win.

I recommend picking the start of a fresh week if you're doing a 1-3 week duration. If you're aiming for a full month, then you may want to start on the first day of the next month.

This is semi-arbitrary, but it helps to have the feeling of a "fresh start" when you initiate a new plan or goal (similar to how people set big life goals on New Year's Eve, right before a new year begins).

However, if you have the energy and motivation to get started now, then go! Start tomorrow if you're ready.

Part II:

Your Money Framework

Chapter 4

Burn Your Ships: Failure is NOT an Option

"I have been impressed with the urgency of doing. Knowing is not enough; we must apply. Being willing is not enough; we must do."
— LEONARDO DA VINCI

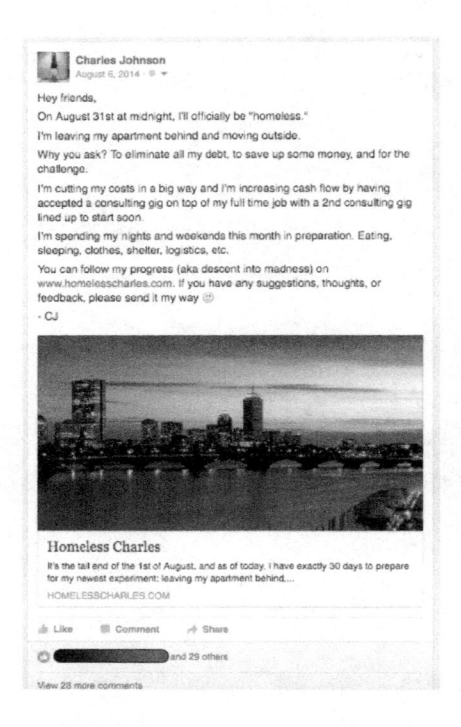

> **Charles Johnson**
> August 6, 2014
>
> Hey friends,
>
> On August 31st at midnight, I'll officially be "homeless."
>
> I'm leaving my apartment behind and moving outside.
>
> Why you ask? To eliminate all my debt, to save up some money, and for the challenge.
>
> I'm cutting my costs in a big way and I'm increasing cash flow by having accepted a consulting gig on top of my full time job with a 2nd consulting gig lined up to start soon.
>
> I'm spending my nights and weekends this month in preparation. Eating, sleeping, clothes, shelter, logistics, etc.
>
> You can follow my progress (aka descent into madness) on www.homelesscharles.com. If you have any suggestions, thoughts, or feedback, please send it my way ☺
>
> - CJ
>
> **Homeless Charles**
> It's the tail end of the 1st of August, and as of today, I have exactly 30 days to prepare for my newest experiment: leaving my apartment behind....
> HOMELESSCHARLES.COM
>
> 👍 Like 💬 Comment ↗ Share
>
> ⬤ and 29 others
> View 28 more comments

I still remember the hesitation I felt right after writing this post. It was a cool night in early August, and I was sitting in my apartment living room in Boston.

How would people react? Would they support me? Or would people think this was stupid, selfish, or inappropriate?

I clicked "Post" and waited.

A minute passed. Five minutes. Ten minutes. Still no reaction. Maybe it wasn't a big deal. Maybe I'd simply built this up too much in my head.

And then the comments started coming in.

"I'm intrigued"

"I think you've gone off your rocker. Please call"

"This is very Thoreau of you"

"Charlie: don't do it. That's my advice."

"If you don't grow an absolutely ridiculous beard, I'll be disappointed."

A CEO of a Google Ventures company responded: "You are absolutely insane and it's awesome. Well done, sir. Excited to follow along!"

Thirty comments later and the verdict was in: overwhelmingly, people supported my plan and thought it was a little bit crazy, but a lot a bit awesome.

I'd just made a public commitment to ditch my apartment and pay off my debt. There was no turning back now.

I'd be lying if I told you I wasn't just a little bit scared, but more than anything I felt invigorated. I had a big goal in front of me, but I was going to tackle it one small step at a time and prove to my friends, my family, and most of all myself, that I could do this.

Burn Your Ships and The Point of No Return

The concept of "burning your ships" dates back to 1519, when Hernan Cortes arrived in the New World. After arriving, Cortes literally burned his ships to prevent retreat. He was sending a clear message to his men: there is no turning back. Within two years, he and his men had conquered the Aztec empire.

Cortes had created a point of no return: a point at which one must continue forward, because turning back is either impossible, too dangerous, or too costly. By burning his ships, Cortes was leaving no room for failure. He and his men would either succeed in conquering the Aztecs, or die trying. The option to retreat no longer existed.

This is an incredibly powerful motivator. If your only options are to conquer the enemy or die, you're going to grab that sword and go conquer something – or literally die trying.

Luckily, your enemy isn't an army of bloodthirsty Aztec warriors (unless you *really* owe money to the wrong people), but it is still a dangerous and insidious foe that you must destroy if you wish to be free.

The Hidden Strength of Public Commitments

When I posted that message on Facebook, I was making a public commitment that I would leave my apartment behind to pay off my debt. I had effectively told hundreds of people about my goal to become debt free and my plan to achieve it.

When you make a public commitment, you unleash a psychological force that comes straight from our evolutionarily honed biology. As a social species, our ability to trade, cooperate, communicate, and live together is all dependent on trust.

When you make a commitment to someone, that person will expect you to follow through on your commitment. Of course, should you "break your word" and not follow through, the person will no longer trust you as much as they did before. Your "word" is no longer as valuable as it once was.

This social capital is a valuable resource, and we are biologically programmed to want to maintain it. And because this desire is hardwired into us, you can leverage it to achieve your goals.

You don't need to post on Facebook to accomplish this next Action Step. You don't even have to tell a bunch of people. You need only share your goal (to become debt free) with one other person who you trust.

Public = at least one other person knows about it.

Commitment = a statement of what you are going to do, how you are going to do it, and when you'll have it done by.

If you're having doubts about this step, that's natural. It's OK to be nervous or think that this step isn't for you. But let me ask you this, do you REALLY want to be debt free? How badly? Is this something you truly care about?

Because if it is, then you should be willing to consider unusual ways to accomplish your goal, right?

If you're right now thinking: "Hell no! There is NO WAY I'm going to talk about my debt situation with someone or make it public knowledge" – I don't blame you.

This step is a hard one for most people. In our society, we rarely talk about the state of our finances, even with close relatives. In fact, most Americans would rather discuss religion, politics, or even DEATH rather than broach the subject of their finances, according to a study from Wells Fargo.

But take a second to think about your Debt Freedom Purpose.

Is this step *really* that difficult given the importance of your greater reason for achieving freedom?

And also remember: the harder it seems, the more momentum you will build if you pull this off.

When I was in debt, I did everything I could to avoid thinking about my finances. I had to give myself a pep talk every time I went to check how much money I had in the bank, and I'd often break out in cold sweats while logging in to my online accounts.

I felt like my life was totally out of control and I hated it. I couldn't stand the thought that while I was suffering the anxiety and frustrations of debt, people in financial institutions were making loads of money through the interest fees they charged me.

I'm recommending this step because I know it can help you. It certainly helped me. What's the worst that could happen?

ACTION STEP 4: Make a Public Commitment

1. Decide on a commitment to make.

The power of "burning your ships" and making a public commitment comes from stating your goal clearly to others, such that if you do not follow through, you will "lose face" with the people you made the commitment to.

The power does not come from the SIZE of the commitment, so it's OK to start with a small commitment now and make bigger commitments later.

I don't recommend starting with a huge, incredible commitment like:

> *"I'm going to pay off all $45,000 of student loan debt within six months."*

Instead, consider beginning with a commitment like this:

> *"I'm going to pay off $1,000 of student loan debt within the next two months."*

Only you can be the judge of how big the commitment should be, but like your quick win challenge, you should make a commitment that you have a good chance of following through on.

PRO TIP: If you haven't finished your quick win challenge yet, combine your public commitment with your quick win to get things really going.

When I started telling people that I was going to pay off all my credit card debt before the end of 2014 (which gave me less than four months), I was comfortable making the commitment because I knew I could do it. It wasn't going to be easy, it would take a lot of sacrifice and hustle, but I knew it was possible.

How did I know this? First, I created a spreadsheet and listed out all the expenses I would have while I was living without a home. I then compared that to my income (and some expected income from side gigs) to get an idea of how much money I'd have available to throw at debt each month.

Based on those calculations, I knew I'd have to come up with some extra cash each month – a sizable amount actually – but I knew I had a reasonably good chance of making it happen.

So for this first public commitment (again, you can make more commitments later), pick something manageable.

2. Decide how you will make it "public."

Again, this doesn't need to be an announcement to the world. If you'd prefer to keep your money situation private, then confide in a close friend or family member. If you're more of an "open book" sort of person, by all means, consider the world (or your Twitter followers) your audience.

Here are some audiences to consider:

- You could tell a trusted friend
- You could share this with your significant other or spouse
- You could post this on Facebook, Twitter, or some other social media channel

Ultimately, this Action Step is about accountability. Whoever you share your commitment with is going to know what you're working on, and this will help you work harder and resist the urge to give up. If failure would be embarrassing, that's a good thing.

You want the pain of NOT following through to be greater than the pain of doing it. Now that's motivation!

Some other things you might consider:

- Create a blog or Twitter account where you will share progress updates
- Start or join a mastermind group focused on money or debt
- Find an accountability partner or coach who will check in on you consistently

Don't spend too much time deliberating over this step, just do a quick "gut check" to see what you are comfortable with and take action fast. But don't forget, when you post something on the internet, it's there forever, so don't say anything you wouldn't want you grandmother to hear. (I've made this mistake before.)

3. Burn your ships.

It's time to post, tweet, share, call, email, text, or do whatever it is you're going to do to make your commitment known to at least one other person.

This might be difficult for you, but if you've thought through steps 1 and 2, then you should be ready for this. Go ahead and light the fire: it's time to burn your ships.

Once you do this, there's no going back. You WILL rise to the challenge and complete your commitment. You WILL do whatever it takes to successfully achieve your goal.

If you need a boost of adrenaline to push the "GO" button on this step, watch a short video or two from my Debt Motivation page that I created just for readers of this book: www.debtdestroyerbook.com/motivation

Go do it. I'll wait. Once you've taken the plunge, move on to the next page.

Congratulations! You've taken a huge step forward by creating an environment that will drive you towards success.

This is a HUGE win, so make sure to take a moment to celebrate what you've just done!

When you look back on this down the road, you will see how instrumental this was in getting you closer to debt freedom.

Chapter 5

Figure Out Where You Stand: The Debt Tracker

"The curious paradox is that when I accept myself just as I am, then I can change."
— CARL ROGERS

Let's take a quick look at what you've already accomplished.

First, you took ownership of your debt situation. Then, you found a powerful motivator to keep you going. Next, you got (or are currently getting) a quick win to jump-start your momentum.

And you just now made a public commitment to hold you accountable.

You've made excellent progress and we're full steam ahead towards debt freedom!

Now it's time to get your hands dirty – to really push forward and get this momentum train moving. It's time to face your debt head on. We're going to figure out exactly how bad your debt situation is.

This step may be emotionally taxing, but to eliminate your debt, you first need to know how much you have.

If you're right now on the verge of a panic attack – it's OK!

Take a deep breath, step away from the book for a second, and give yourself a chance to come to grips with the situation. We're simply going to gather some numbers together and write them down.

Whatever you do, DO NOT tell yourself you'll do this later. Do this NOW while you're reading this. You can take a break and reward yourself afterwards, but you must do this now.

Do you want to remember (for the rest of your life) how you gave up just when things got a little tough?

Or do you want to look back on today as the day you started to kick debt's ass?

ACTION STEP 5: Create Your Debt Tracker
Time to Complete: 20 Minutes

1. Download the Debt Tracker template file.

I want this to be as painless as possible for you, so I've already created a spreadsheet template that you can download and use to quickly track your debt.

Go to www.debtdestroyerbook.com/step1 to download it now.

2. List out ALL of your debts.

Now list out every single debt you have: the name of the lender (the company you owe money), the type of debt (eg., student loan, credit card #1, etc.), and a link to your login page (or other contact info – anything that helps you stay organized).

The order of your debts doesn't matter yet, just make sure you aren't missing anything. If you're not exactly sure what debts you have, go through your mail, emails, and voicemails and see if there's anything else you can add to the list.

3. Figure out how much you owe for each debt.

Now the hard part. For each one, you need to figure out four things:

- Exactly how much you owe
- When the next payment is due
- What the minimum payment is
- What your interest rate is

Log into online portals, make calls to lenders, or open your unopened mail to find the latest statement. Whatever you need to do to find this information – do it now. Make sure you're looking at the most up to date information. You don't want any surprises later.

This is a short chapter for a reason. For most people, looking up debt amounts and interest rates is a pain in the ass and requires a good deal of willpower. I know it's not fun to be reminded of how much debt you have, but this step is absolutely necessary.

I'll say this one last time: do this NOW!

You may be tempted to take a break or write this step down as a "to do" and deal with it later, but you need to resist the urge and instead push forward. Do whatever you need to do to make this happen right now: drink a cup of coffee, turn up the music, slap yourself in the face a couple times… whatever it takes.

Complete this (admittedly unpleasant) step now.

Done?

OK, so you've finished. You now have a complete list of all your debts (student loans, credit cards, auto loans, mortgage, medical debt, etc.).

Give yourself a well-deserved pat on the back, and treat yourself to a celebratory reward for your hard work (personally, I like the combo of Netflix with chips and hummus).

I'm sure this wasn't fun, but you're now ready to move on to the next important part of the process. If this step exhausted your willpower for the day, feel free to put the book down and start the next chapter tomorrow. You've earned it.

Meet Jesse

Junior year of college was when things really began to set in. I was changing my major for the second time and the process opened up my eyes to what I was paying for my education. It was easy to ignore while being a student, but I had about a year and a half left until I had to start paying back my student loans. I had $135,000 of debt to my name. Staying an extra semester and going to an out of state school didn't help.

I thought that my loan payments after college would be reasonable. I was wrong. My student loan payments are $1,500/month. I have a good job which helps, but that's still a lot of debt for one person to handle.

I think about my student loan debt every single day. It makes me anxious knowing I owe SO much money. I used to feel trapped and depressed. I wanted to ignore the situation, but the truth is, ignoring debt is almost impossible and doing so doesn't make it go away. I had to make a change for my own sanity and happiness, and to live the life I want.

The first thing I knew I had to do was write down all my expenses along with my income and figure out where my money was going. I looked at places where I could cut back and save. The expenses that stood out to me were my phone bill, car payment and car insurance. My phone bill was $120/month for a nice smartphone and 10 gigs of data. Did I need that? No. Did I want it, well, yes, but not as much as I wanted to get out of debt, so I switched to a prepaid monthly phone plan and got a cheaper phone that I paid outright. Now, my bill is $45/month.

Next, I realized I was paying $450/month for a car payment and about $115/month for car insurance. I traded in my car and got a leased hybrid car. I renegotiated my car insurance payment as well. That saved me a total of $120/month including the reduced gas expense as I was mostly driving on electric and it was much cheaper to fill up.

The next few things I did REALLY helped bring in extra income. I started driving with Uber on weekends. That gave me an extra $400/month to work with. I also bought a house, which has two units. I live in 1 with my brother and rent the other out on Airbnb. The income from Airbnb and the rent collected from my brother pays my entire mortgage, so the money I would have had to spend on a housing situation for myself can go towards my loans. I'm living in a house for free AND I'm making money from it.

I also sell things I'm not using on Craigslist for extra cash and shop at the Salvation Army if I need new clothes. Some folks look down on shopping for used items instead of new, but I'm not ashamed. I look at it as recycling and I'm helping others who need it rather that a big corporation.

After some advice from Charlie, I took a look at the student loans I had left, figured out which had the smallest balances and which charged the most interest and prioritized them to pay them down fast. I use Simple bank which lets me create goals for my loans and when I'd like to pay them off by, then my bank puts that money aside for me so I don't have to think about it. I've already paid off 2 loans totaling around 15K and I'm due to pay off a loan with a 5K balance off in about 6 months.

My advice to you is to not hide from your debt. Lay out all of your expenses and income. Be disciplined about where your money is going and set goals for yourself. Sell things you don't need and look for side gigs you can do. Also, check to see if your bank has a feature where they can put money aside for you, or switch to a bank that can. That feature alone has helped me save up and pay off several important expenses in my life. Make a plan, stick to it, and you'll be okay. :)
- Jesse Bentsen

Chapter 6

Taking Massive Action: Airbnb and Sleeping in the Woods

"Make no little plans; they have no magic to stir men's blood and probably themselves will not be realized."
— DANIEL BURNHAM

"You're crazy, man... you can't do this!"

My friend thought I was nuts for wanting to sleep outside to save money. Honestly, I couldn't blame him: it was an unusual approach to say the least.

For the first half hour of our conversation, he tried to persuade me to keep my apartment. He warned me about the possibility of physical dangers (I could be attacked in my sleep), of the law (it wasn't legal), and of my future (how would people react to such a thing?) – he was worried this was going too far and would do more harm than good.

But his tune slowly changed as I explained my plan to him.

I shared the work I'd done so far:

- Recon missions into woodland and wildlife areas around the city
- Research into potential legal consequences should I get caught
- Testing the social waters by throwing it into conversation with friends and acquaintances

I'd even created a nutrition plan that would keep my immune system strong enough to handle the incoming cold weather (we were on the verge of another freezing Boston winter). This healthy diet would also help me deal with the inevitable lack of sleep from early mornings and late nights.

He was resistant at first, by the end of the conversation my friend wanted to join me. He still thought it was crazy, but his perspective had changed. It was no longer the ill-conceived schemes of a crazy person. Now he saw it as an adventure he wanted to be a part of – he even wanted to go sleep out in the woods too.

Fast forward to two years later.

I'm on the rooftop deck of a hotel in Ho Chi Minh City, Vietnam meeting with entrepreneurs to discuss emerging trends and startup best practices.

"You did what?"

Someone had mentioned their debt, and we'd swapped debt-payoff stories. As soon as it got out that I'd slept in the woods to pay off debt, the group's conversation switched gears. The talk of email marketing tactics and conversion rate optimization quieted down as I began fielding questions from all sides of the table:

"How did you shower?"

"Where did you keep your things?"

"What did you do to make money on the side?"

If you'd asked me two years ago what I thought people would find interesting about me, it certainly wouldn't have been sleeping in the woods to pay off my debt. It's not that I'm ashamed or embarrassed about it – on the contrary, I'm proud of my four month journey living without a home. I just didn't think it would resonate with so many people.

As it turns out, my experience in the woods was not only a lesson in how to pay off debt fast, but a lesson in human psychology. Making big, bold, ambitious plans is exciting. It gets you fired up!

I can't even begin to describe how excited I was to leave my apartment on the last day before I moved outside – I felt truly, utterly, alive. For so many people, life is a series of not-so-exciting events, so when something different, unique, and daring comes along, it gets attention.

And now it's your turn. I want YOU to think big too.

I'm not going to ask you to sleep outside, in the woods, or under your desk at work.

I'd probably get in trouble for recommending those things, so I explicitly do not recommend or condone doing any of those things. But... let me know if you decide to do any of those things and we'll talk about it (contact info at the end of the book).

Your biggest expense is probably rent. So I encourage you to at least consider how you could take massive action on that front.

Could you Airbnb your place out from time to time?
Could you break your lease and move somewhere cheaper?
Could you get someone else to move in and split the bill?
Could you couch surf indefinitely?
Could you move back home with your parents (or in with a friend) for a few months?

If you can't take action on the home front, consider other areas of your life. But whatever you do, don't settle.

Sleeping in the woods (or under your desk at the office), might be too extreme, but what about using Airbnb to make some cash every now and then?

Before ditching my apartment, I tried to monetize it.

I signed up for Airbnb, had a professional photographer stop by to get well-lit shots, and even invested $600 in making the place look nice. I'd done my research and found that the places that were making real money were the ones with a bunch of good reviews.

It's hard to get started on Airbnb without any ratings or positive feedback, so I was going to have to find a way to break my way into the already crowded Airbnb market in Boston.

To get my first customers, I spiffed up my apartment with furnishings from Bed Bath & Beyond and lowered my per night price to well below market average. It worked – I had requests coming in fast.

Unfortunately, my landlord made a habit of scanning the local Airbnb listings to look for signs of his properties, and lo and behold, there was my apartment.

I cancelled my Airbnb listing after receiving a message threatening legal action (I was breaking the terms of my lease), but this doesn't mean you can't take advantage of Airbnb, or a similar renting service.

If you have a spare room, rent it out! Or maybe crash at a friend's place every now and then while you rent out your entire place. Maybe this will work for you, or maybe it's not a good fit.

The purpose of this chapter is to get you to think beyond the obvious.

Yes, cutting back on Starbucks and food truck lunches can help, but one single consulting check or Airbnb payment could be worth 10X whatever money you save from little daily sacrifices.

Remember the 80/20 rule: you'll get most of your results from just a few key actions, so use your limited willpower on the things that really make a difference, and think big.

This might sound contrary to what we talked about with progressive escalation and celebrating small wins in the last chapter, but it's not. Let me explain.

You absolutely need to break your work into small chunks and move forward incrementally, taking one step at a time. This is crucial to your long-term success. And so is the idea of celebrating small wins along the way. If you don't appreciate your progress, you won't feel like you're progressing and your motivation will suffer.

But here's the kicker: if you don't set ambitious goals – big, bold, daring, inspiring ones – then will you really be motivated to achieve them?

You can have big goals while taking small steps, and that's exactly what I recommend you do.

However you approach the challenge of getting out of debt, I encourage you to explore new, creative, ambitious goals that will galvanize you into action. If you've been in debt for a while now, your motivation might not be as strong as you'd like it to be.

You might be worried that thinking "big" isn't for you – but you're wrong.

Yes, you need to start small – everyone does. But you can, and should, think BIG. If you didn't want to accomplish big goals in the first place, you wouldn't have come this far.

And you're here with me right now. So what does that tell you?

How to Think Big

Find role models.

If you want to think outside the box and get creative with your savings, income, and debt repayment strategy, then find role models who inspire you.

Find people who do big things.

Read about them. Watch videos about them. Learn about them. Find out what motivates them to do what they do.

Tim Ferriss wants to push the limits of what humans are capable of.

Tony Robbins wants to transform people's lives.

Elon Musk wants to save our species and change the course of history.

These people inspire me and encourage me to think big.

Who inspires you?

Keep track of what inspires YOU.

Part of thinking big is being inspired.

I use Evernote to keep track of videos, articles, and quotes that inspire me and motivate me to be better and do more. I recommend you keep track of what inspires you and reference it often.

Check out the stories on www.debtdestroyerbook.com/inspiration to get started.

Chapter 7

Take Control: A 5 Minute Spending Plan

"Did you choose courage, or comfort today?"
– BRENÉ BROWN

Forty-seven dollars.

That's how much my fancy new budgeting app cost me.

I bought it. Installed it. Watched the tutorial videos... and then never used it.

Turns out, budgeting sucks. No one enjoys keeping track of how much they spend. If you happen to be among the 0.001% of people who like this sort of thing, more power to you – but that isn't me.

I bought the budgeting software thinking it would make it easier to track my finances (that's certainly what it promised), but it didn't.

The app wasn't intuitive, it had lots of confusing screens, and it didn't tell me exactly what I needed to do or why I needed to do it.

And for something like budgeting – something I already have to PUSH myself to do – I needed it to be drop dead simple for me to commit to it, and this was the opposite of simple.

In this chapter, you're going to take control of your money by creating a simple spending plan.

I use the term "spending plan" as opposed to "budget" because these days most people don't know what a budget is. Is it comparing income vs. expenses? Is it a way of tracking expenses as they occur? Or is it a commitment to a monthly amount of spending (whether that actually happens or not)?

A "spending plan," on the other hand, is self-explanatory: it's a plan that represents how you intend to spend your money.

As a bonus, we'll compare your income vs. expenses to see what your cash flow looks like.

If you search online for budgeting apps you'll find plenty: there are websites, smartphone apps, computer programs, PDF templates and online spreadsheets. I'm sure many of them are great. The problem isn't that they all suck (although many of them do) – the problem is that there are too many options.

Instead of trying to find a robust, fully-featured budgeting solution (like I originally did), we're going to start with a simple spreadsheet.

Download the template file here:
www.debtdestroyerbook.com/step1

This spending plan will give you 100% clarity on where your money is going each month. Once you finish putting your numbers in, this plan will tell you:

- How much money you have coming in (income)
- How much money is going out (expenses)
- The difference between the two (is there anything left over after expenses?)

Setting this up might sound like a massive task, but it's a lot easier than you'd think.

And once you've finished filling out the plan, you'll be firmly standing at the helm of your financial ship. When you know exactly where your money is going, it becomes MUCH easier to figure out what to do next.

We'll go through the steps necessary to create your 5 Minute Spending Plan in just a minute, but first consider the following.

Day to Day Tracking

Your spending plan is like a blueprint for your money: it's where your dollars and cents should go.

Where they actually go in the real world likely differs.

You need to create a Spending Plan to figure out your cash flow and start to figure out where your money is going, but if you want to get data-driven and track where your money goes on a day-to-day level, you'll need a little more.

There are three options I want you to consider. Pick whichever one seems more convenient to you.

They all accomplish the same thing: they let you know exactly how much you can afford to spend, so before you pull the trigger on that Americano at Starbucks, you can use the tool, make a conscious decision, and get back to your life – all in seconds.

The Envelope Method

The envelope method has been around for decades and is a bullet-proof system for clamping down on overspending and forcing the spender to pay more attention to everyday purchases.

It works like this:

1. Get a handful of envelopes.

You're going to need one envelope for each common spending category (like groceries, dining out, entertainment, etc.). Label each envelope with the name of the type of expense you want to track, like "Groceries."

2. Withdraw cash for each spending category.

Let's say you plan for $400 worth of grocery expenses each month. If you get a paycheck twice a month, then withdraw $200 from your first paycheck (or direct deposit) to have enough cash for groceries until your second paycheck arrives – then pull out another $200 in cash to cover groceries for the rest of the month. Withdraw enough cash to cover each category you're tracking and keep the bills separate in their respective envelopes.

If you get paid on a different schedule, say, once a month, pull out enough cash to cover your expenses until the next paycheck.

3. Spend money from your envelopes.

Keep these envelopes with you throughout the day. If you need to tuck them into your wallet, purse, messenger bag, backpack, briefcase, etc. – do it.

Keeping the money separate makes it easier to see how much you're spending on different types of purchases. As the days go by, you'll notice yourself paying more attention to what you're buying and for how much. At some point, you might notice that you're running out of money in one envelope or another – that's OK. You might run out of money earlier than expected – it happens, especially when you're just getting started with this system.

Try to resist the urge to cheat on your envelopes by borrowing cash from one to pay for another – that makes it too easy to say you're going to spend $100 on clothing this month, and then instead spend $150.

Instead, try to stretch your dollars for as long as you can and try to make it to the next paycheck, when you'll withdraw more cash.

If you come up way short, you may need to reevaluate your spending plan. That's fine too: you don't need to get it 100% right the first time.

I recommend using the envelope system for all spending categories that lend themselves to cash payments. You probably can't pay cash for your rent or mortgage payments, and your lenders aren't likely to accept bills for debt repayments either. Just focus on what you can, and remember – whatever amount of money you allot for a given spending category should stay in that envelope.

One last point: you're spending cash only for these categories – NO CREDIT OR DEBIT CARDS.

YNAB: You Need A Budget

Another great option for tracking your money – one that's like the envelope method but without physical envelopes – is YNAB: You Need A Budget. It's a budgeting app originally built by a guy who was just trying to create a system for tracking his and his wife's money – but it has since evolved into a full-fledged online money tracking tool that anyone can use.

YNAB comes in two flavors (you get both): the website and the mobile app. Both allow you to track your spending by entering in new transactions as they happen in real-time.

You can use YNAB for several things, but I've found it to be immensely valuable for two key purposes:

1. Allocating money to your spending categories (do this every time you get paid)

2. Seeing how much money you still have available to spend on something without going over your planned spending

After years of only using a spreadsheet spending plan, I just recently upgraded to YNAB. Their latest version costs $5/month, but I think it's well worth it.

Anytime I'm about to purchase something, whether online or in-person, I check my YNAB app to see how much money I have available for that type of purchase. If I'm running low on allotted cash, I might change my mind and skip the purchase (or look for alternatives). And anytime I pull the trigger and buy something, I make a quick entry in the app to record it.

I thought it would be tedious having to update the app every time I spend money, but after one week using the app I was hooked. Now I don't even think about it; I just do it.

When you can see your spending in real time (and see how much money you have left to spend), you're much more likely to...

- Avoid impulse purchases because you checked your tracker first
- Consciously purchase something (without needing to feel guilty) because it was part of your planned spending
- Recognize the things that matter most to you and start thinking about how to use your money to serve you best

If you'd rather not spend money on the tool you're using for saving money (totally understandable), then consider using...

Mint.com

A free and easy to use money tracking service from Intuit. This will show you where your money is going and allows you to quickly check your money situation.

You don't have to use the envelope method or YNAB (or any other money tracking app) to successfully take control of your money – but tools like these can help.

If you're not sure what you want to do, skip these for now and consider them later after you've progressed through the rest of the book.

Finally, remember that your money victories won't always be financial. Sometimes they're behavioral, psychological, or emotional. A better night's sleep, less stress throughout the day, a sense of control over your life... these are real, tangible results worth achieving – and worth celebrating.

OK, let's create your spending plan already.

Go to www.debtdestroyer.com/tools to find the links for these trackers.

ACTION STEP 6: Create Your Spending Plan

We've talked about it. Now it's time to do it.

1. List out all your income.

Using the Companion Guide you downloaded, write in the name and amount of all your monthly income sources. This includes salary/wages, any part-time job income, freelance income, commission checks, as well as alimony and child support. Any money that's flowing into your pockets, wallet, or bank account goes on here.

2. List out all your expenses.

Now do the same thing with all your expenses for a typical month. In addition to including things like rent, groceries, your cell phone, internet, etc. – also account for your minimum payments on all your debt. Go back to the Debt Tracker spreadsheet you completed and copy/paste the minimums.

Obviously, you don't want to fall behind on your payments (credit card companies in particular can charge you higher "penalty" interest rates if you miss a payment – not fun), so we're going to count the minimum payments as part of your expected spending for each month.

OPTIONAL 7 Day Challenge: To get accurate figures for how much you spend on things like groceries, dining out, entertainment, etc., consider tracking your spending for 7 days (if you already did this as your Quick Win challenge, great!)

For just one full week, keep a pen and slip of paper with you at all times. Don't try to budget, just observe what you purchase and make note of it. Alternatively, you can link your credit cards to

Mint.com. Mint will automatically track your spending for you and put it into a nifty pie chart.

Whatever you do, try to get accurate numbers for your expenses – don't just guess. People are notoriously bad at guessing how much money they spend each month (myself included) and creating your spending plan with real numbers will allow you to start making thoughtful, powerful changes to your plan.

This is optional! Don't bite off more than you can chew. But if you're up to it, do this now and then finish creating this plan when you're done.

3. Compare your income vs. expenses.

Now that you have an accurate and complete list of all your income and all your regular monthly expenses, it's time to see where you stand from a cash flow perspective. What direction is the money flowing? Are you in the red: spending more than you earn? Or are you in the black: making more than you spend?

If you're currently "cash flow negative," meaning you spend more than you earn, then it's time to make a change, and quick.

In your current situation, you are going to dig yourself deeper and deeper into debt as the months go by. Time is working against you until you fix your cash flow problem.

The remainder of this book will show you how to turn things around and get money flowing in the right direction. Once you are cash flow positive, you'll be able to focus on paying off your debt.

If you're currently "cash flow positive" – meaning you earn more than you spend, congratulations!

You should have money left over at the end of each month. If you're careful with your money, you'll eventually pay off all your debt. The remainder of this book will help you speed things up and pay off your debt faster.

Done with this step? Great. Now that you have a spending plan, you can make more informed financial decisions and keep an eye on your expenses. You've completed the important step of figuring out your cash flow, and this will in turn allow you to create a debt repayment plan in the next chapter.

If you're feeling a little worn down, this is a good time to take a break and celebrate your victory – creating a spending plan probably wasn't fun, but it was a critical step forward towards financial freedom, and you've proven yourself capable once again.

Chapter 8

Where to Start: A 3 Minute Debt Elimination System

"The greatest danger never lies in setting our aim too high and falling short, but aiming too low and achieving our mark."
– MICHELANGELO

You know where you stand with your debt thanks to your Debt Tracker. You know what's going on with your money thanks to your Spending Plan.

Now it's time to figure out how to pay off your debt once and for all. We're going to create a plan that will tell you exactly how much money to put towards which debt, when.

Your debt elimination system will do three important things:

- **Allow you to see PROGRESS.** For every debt you pay off, you get to cross it off the list. The more progress you make, the more debts crossed off. It's one thing to know you're paying off your debt, it's another to SEE it. This will help you feel the momentum you're building and keep you motivated to continue towards debt freedom.

- **Give you more CONTROL.** Once you create your Debt Elimination System, there's no guesswork in figuring out how much money to put towards your debt, or when to make payments, or which debt to focus on – the system provides answers to all your questions, giving you complete control over your debt.

- **Keep you FOCUSED.** It's easy to get distracted when juggling lots of debt. It's also easy to dilute your efforts by trying to pay off too many debts at the same time. This plan will keep you focused on only the debt that needs to be addressed now.

Create this plan even if your current expenses outweigh your income.

If you're cash flow negative, you'll first need to plug the holes in your financial boat so you don't sink – but once you're no longer bleeding cash, you'll have this plan ready to put into action.

It won't take more than a few minutes, and forever after you'll feel like an Angel of Debt is watching over you, guiding you toward the light as you... OK I'm gonna stop. This metaphor sucks... moving on.

ACTION STEP 7: Create a Debt Elimination System

1. Download the Debt Elimination Spreadsheet.

It's already set up; you just need to plug in the numbers and it'll calculate everything else for you. Go to www.debtdestroyerbook.com/step1 to get your copy.

2. Figure out how much to put towards debt.

Go back to your spending plan and see how much money you have left over after paying your expenses + minimum payments. If you're cash flow negative, you can skip this and move on to the next step (come back once you've improved your cash flow). If you're cash flow positive, allocate some (or all) of that money to paying off your debt.

3. Arrange your debts by the size of the balance.

Using your Debt Tracker, list out all the debts you have in order from smallest to largest.

4. Put the allocated money towards the 1st debt.

Take aim. The first debt, the one with the lowest balance – this is your target. Whatever amount of money you decided to put towards debt in step 2, goes towards this debt. Set all your other debts to auto-pay the minimum amount.

Seriously, I shouldn't have to say this, but PLEASE use automatic payments: it's one less thing you need to waste your limited energy on. If you don't have this option, no big deal – just keep paying the minimum due manually.

5. Track your progress!

Update how much is left on the 1st debt every time you make a payment.

Humans are wired to focus on short-term gains (as you're about to see with the Marshmallow Experiment in the next chapter). This is one of the reasons it can be hard to stay motivated in the long term.

BUT, there's an easy trick you can use to hijack this quirk of human nature and make it work for you: track your goals so you get immediate feedback. This is why measuring a goal (be it money, weight, or anything else) is so effective – you get to enjoy your gains immediately, even if you haven't hit your final target yet.

How's this for an inspiring sentence: $5,000 $4,000 $2,000 $0

6. Continue to pay the smallest unpaid debt.

Once you pay off the lowest balance debt that you selected in step 4, your next target is the following lowest balance debt, and then the next lowest after that, etc. By always paying the lowest balance debt first, you will get the satisfaction of crossing debts off your list sooner. This will keep you motivated.

Great job. You now have a Debt Elimination System you can reference quickly and manage with just a few minutes every couple weeks. Keep this spreadsheet handy and make a calendar reminder to update it every pay cycle: Get paid, pay off some debt, update the spreadsheet, win.

This system using what is commonly referred to as the "Snowball Method" of debt repayment. It's another principle from the world of finance that's been around for decades and as you can see, it's pretty straightforward. By paying down your smallest debts first, you'll keep the momentum going with small wins along the path to debt freedom – this keeps you energized and motivated.

Full disclosure: There is a mathematically more efficient debt elimination method that could save you a little more money (you'll pay less in interest fees) – if you can stick to it. The trade-off is motivation. This other plan does not necessarily help you stay motivated.

I strongly recommend you stick with the Snowball Method that we've just used to create our Debt Elimination System, but I'll explain the other method in the last chapter at the end of this book in case you're interested.

My reasoning for this is simple: *the imperfect plan you stick with is infinitely better than the perfect plan you abandon.*

Pay Off Debt App

Did you read through this chapter with no intention of creating a Debt Elimination System? I hope not, but if you're looking for something easier, then there's another option you should consider.

Download the Pay Off Debt app for iPhone and Android.

It's not free, it costs $5 as of this writing, but it's one of the best apps I've seen for strategically managing your debt repayments. After being featured in Oprah's magazine, this app's popularity has really taken off. (I mean come on, if Oprah likes it…)

You can check it out here: www.debtdestroyerbook.com/tools

Part III:
Incredible Profitability

Chapter 9

Everything Popular is Wrong: Save Money Like Warren Buffett

"Too many people spend money they earned to buy things they don't want to impress people that they don't like."
— WILL ROGERS

Spinach, kale, Brussels sprouts, chard, blackberries, cranberries, smoked salmon and a sprinkling of flaxseed and cinnamon, drenched in olive oil – that was my breakfast almost every morning.

I'd come back from Trader Joe's with a HUGE brown bag full of healthy goodies. The irony was that this was part of my new spending plan – my plan to save money. Yet here I was, buying organic veggies and expensive add-ons. And the premium health food didn't end there: my lunch usually involved quinoa, mixed nuts, and hard-boiled eggs or chicken breast.

Since I prepared all my meals in the office, my colleagues would sometimes question me about it. I'd often get asked: "how can you afford all this?"

What they really wanted to know was, how could I afford all this on a tight budget?

When presented with the concept of saving money, most people immediately jump to the notion of cutting back on all expenses, eliminating the morning Starbucks, and making sacrifices now in order to enjoy a better future later. The problem with this model of saving is that as human beings, we are notoriously bad at making short-term sacrifices to enjoy long-term rewards.

Take the Marshmallow Experiment.

Back in the 60s there was an experiment at Stanford University by researcher Walter Mischel, who wanted to understand at what age the ability to defer gratification developed in children.

Children between the ages of four to six were individually led into an empty room and given a treat (e.g., a marshmallow). Before eating the treat, the children were told that if they could wait fifteen minutes without giving into temptation, they would be given a second treat in addition to the first.

So, the question was: would the child eat one treat now, or wait it out and have two treats in fifteen minutes?

The results were hilarious – and extremely revealing of human nature. The vast majority of children *attempted* to wait out the fifteen minutes to get two treats. However, of those that tried to defer gratification, only one third actually made it the full fifteen minutes without giving in and eating the treat.

As human beings, we are wired to take advantage of pleasures in the here and now. Maybe it's because for most of our existence as a species, pleasures were short-lived and unpredictable.

The figs on the tree weren't going to last long – birds or other animals would get to them fast – so it made sense to go to town and eat as many as you could in one sitting. With resources hard to come by, it's better to overeat and accumulate calories – which could later be burned during times of scarcity – rather than eat a balanced meal.

This extends beyond food. When faced with the option of enjoying a couple hours of Netflix versus reading an educational book, many would prefer the former, even if they feel guilty about it.

This difficulty with sacrificing doesn't mean we're bad people, and it doesn't make us immoral. It just means we're human.

Our brains have evolved over a long period of time, and we aren't fully equipped to deal with a digital age full of advertising, temptations, and an abundance of food and entertainment options – it's all very new.

It's OK if you're not great at making sacrifices or cutting back. Most people aren't.

I've struggled with the dilemma of saving money myself. There are plenty of things I'd like to spend my money on: healthy food, dining out, renting movies, nutritional supplements... the list goes on, and the temptation is all too real.

So what does all of this have to do with my healthy salads and spending money on organic vegetables while I'm supposed to be cutting back? Well, it turns out the dilemma of sacrificing now vs. enjoying the present is a false dichotomy.

In other words, you can have your cake and eat it too – but there's a catch. Let me explain.

There's a secret to saving money that most people don't know about – and you can use it to enjoy life now, while still tucking money away for the future. It's extremely simple, but must be implemented carefully to work.

The secret is prioritizing your expenses.

Let me ask you a question. Out of everything you spend money on – your rent, utilities, groceries, insurance, cell phone, internet, etc. – which of these expenses make your life more enjoyable and fulfilling?

After all, that is why we spend money on things, right? Money is simply a tool for getting what we want in life, isn't it? We want to be happy now, and we want to know we'll be happy later.

However, not all our purchases contribute equally to our present (or future) happiness.

So ask yourself...

Which of your expenses REALLY contribute to your happiness? Which add to your overall well-being?

And just as importantly... which do not?

As I mentioned before, prioritizing your expenses is a simple concept but implementing it is where the rubber meets the road.

This chapter's Action Step is all about taking your cash flow to the next level by reducing your expenses in a way that doesn't feel like sacrifice.

This may involve some trial and error (and yes, it requires a little willpower up front) but once you set this in motion, you'll find yourself adapting quickly to your new lifestyle, and you'll have more money available for debt payments and the things you really care about.

WARNING: Completing this step could have profound results and dramatically impact your lifestyle. This exercise led to me ditching my apartment and sleeping in the woods for four months.

Always remember that money is just a tool to get you what you want in life. Most of us spend money on things that don't TRULY enrich our lives, yet we think we need them.

This exercise involves some out of the box thinking, so keep an open mind and get ready to get your soul-search on.

ACTION STEP 8: Prioritize Your Expenses

1. Download the Prioritize Your Expenses Worksheet.

You can find it here: http://www.debtdestroyerbook.com/step1. You already have your expenses listed in your Spending Plan, so have that handy too. We're going to examine these in critical detail.

2. Rank your expenses in terms of value.

Using the worksheet, rank your expenses in terms of how important they are to you. Which of these are so important that you could not give them up without taking a big hit to your quality of life? Which of these are nice to have, but you could give up and still be happy?

For each expense, try to imagine life without it. What does that life look like? For instance, eating healthy ranked very high on my list – meanwhile, I realized that having a roof over my head for a few months wasn't critical to my long-term happiness.

3. Identify your top 5 quality of life expenses.

Out of the expenses you ranked highest, which of these are the most important for you to maintain a great quality of life? Are any of these expenses something that you could spend more money on to increase your quality of life?

4. Identify your least valuable expenses.

Out of the expenses you rated lowest, which of these are the least valuable, the least important for you to maintain a great quality of life?

5. Reallocate your money to go to the expenses in order of priority.

You've now effectively prioritized your expenses in terms of their value to you. It's now time to realign your spending with your priorities. Your options include:

- Spending more money on things that will improve your quality of life
- Spending less money on things that add little to your life
- Eliminating the lowest contributing expenses

Of course, there is a fourth option. You could do nothing at all. You might find that you're 100% satisfied with the way you're spending your money.

This exercise is intended to make you more aware of your spending and how aligned (or misaligned) your expenses are in regards to your priorities. You now have the information in front of you. What you do now is in your hands.

If your morning latte from Starbucks is something you crave and enjoy, then so be it. Tell the penny pinchers to screw off and go enjoy your latte. If paying for your gym membership helps you stay positive and de-stress after work, then great, keep pumping iron.

Keep the expenses that are most important, then whip out the chainsaw and get brutal with everything else.

If you're like me, I think you'll find you are spending money on many things that on the surface seem like they make you happy, but when you dig a little deeper, you realize they don't add much value (or even *detract* from your quality of life).

When I went through this exercise two years ago, I realized that while I thought having a one-bedroom apartment to myself made me happy, I depended much more on my sense of fitness and health.

My quality of life may have benefited slightly from having the bachelor pad, but it benefited far more from eating healthy food and exercising regularly. When I discovered this, the question of what to cut from my life to save money and pay off debt faster suddenly had a clear answer. I didn't need my apartment to maintain my quality of life, so I got rid of it.

Even if you're fairly satisfied with your current spending, I challenge you to change something.

It's very unlikely that the way you spend your money today is 100% in line with your values and your priorities.

Cutting costs and saving more money (that can be put towards your debt) DOES NOT have to feel like sacrifice. If you spend less on the things that don't matter, and spend the same (or even more!) on the things that do, you'll get the positive benefit of saving money without feeling like you have to scrimp and be hyper-frugal.

Chapter 10

Winning the Money Game: Naming Porn Flicks and Selling Restaurants

"Opportunity is missed by most people because it is dressed in overalls and looks like work."
– THOMAS EDISON

I tore the page out of the magazine and held it up. "That'll be $5."

We were in middle school, out in the campus between classes, and I was selling pornography (I know: we grow up so fast these days. At least I was in a growth industry).

He handed over a five-dollar bill and I gave him the page. On it was a young woman in a bikini.

My customers were pubescent teenage boys from my classes. My inventory was a Maxim magazine I'd found at a retail supermarket.

I can still remember walking through the store after school one day and finding myself in the magazine section. I was looking at video game magazines, when something struck my eye: the adult section. I didn't want to get caught looking through the magazines, so I grabbed the nearest one, along with a couple of game magazines and headed for the checkout aisle.

Of all the checkout lanes, somehow I ended up with a sweet looking old woman for my cashier.

My heart started beating faster as I approached the front of the line. I moved the adult magazine in between my two gamer magazines, thinking maybe she'd just scan them all quickly without noticing it. Then it was my turn. I set the magazines down, grabbed a couple candy bars from the candy rack, hoping they might help distract her, and then awaited my fate.

Without hesitation, the woman reached straight for my magazines, separated them, and then immediately held up the adult magazine. I instantly flushed red in the face – and then almost choked on my breath as she opened the magazine and started scanning from page to page.

Was it illegal for me to purchase this? Was I about to get in serious trouble?

Thoughts of police officers arresting me for "attempt to purchase pornography" crossed my young adolescent mind as I watched in horror while the cashier carefully examined each page of the magazine. It was too late to turn back, and I didn't dare turn around to face the line of people undoubtedly watching the entertainment from behind me.

"Well, it's not actually a magazine, so I can't sell it to you," she finally muttered as she set it down and went back to scanning my other items.

Huh? I didn't understand. Was she going to take it away from me? Was I in trouble? I didn't know what she meant by that. She put the magazines – all of them – in a bag with the candy, then handed it to me with my change.

"Have a good day."

And with that, she turned to the next customer.

For a few seconds, I just stood there, stunned and confused. Then I came back to reality and bolted out of the store, embarrassed and worried that someone might have recognized me during this fiasco.

When I'd walked a couple blocks away from the store, I opened my bag to find the adult magazine. Turning it over, I discovered what the cashier had meant. It wasn't the regular Maxim magazine sold in stores, it was a promotional version – and because of this she hadn't charged me for it. I'd been given it for free. As a young naive teenager, I felt like I'd gotten away with murder.

Back to the middle school campus.

Showing the Maxim magazine to my friends, I quickly discovered that there was a lot of demand to see the pictures, even if the women inside didn't reveal any nudity. The kids in my classes didn't have access to this type of stuff (at least not the kids who I talked with) so the demand was high and supply was low. The opportunity finally clicked when one kid offered to pay me for a picture. I was in business.

It wasn't long before my pockets were full of candy (kids without money traded me Skittles and Snickers bars instead) and dollar bills. The best part? I felt powerful. I felt in control. I felt like the master of my destiny.

As someone who'd grown up playing computer and video games, I loved the feeling of "winning." There's nothing quite like successfully overcoming a difficult challenge and reaping the rewards, and with this new business I experienced the same feeling I enjoyed when beating a level in a difficult game: that feeling of accomplishment, of success, of winning.

It didn't take long before I'd recruited a fellow classmate to source new inventory and began tearing pictures out of school magazines. Anything that showed a beautiful woman was fair game: kids would buy pictures even if they were from an ad in a fashion magazine.

I almost didn't include this story, since I wasn't planning on sharing this with my parents (sorry, Mom!) – but I decided it was worth it to give you a sense of how addicting making money on the side can become. This is a good thing – though maybe don't adopt my exact business model.

When you get a taste of success from a side gig, or an online business, you'll get hooked and want to grow it and make it into something more. Consider yourself warned.

ACTION STEP 9: Increase Your Income

When it comes to making money, there are a lot of different paths to choose from.

- If you already have a full-time job, you could negotiate a raise.
- If you are currently doing part-time work, you could transition to full-time.
- If your company doesn't pay that much (or won't let you advance), you could leverage your current job to get a higher paying one somewhere else.
- You could do freelance work on the side.
- You could take a nights-and-weekends job.

In this chapter, we'll consider all of these paths and more.

Where there's a will there's a way, and if you're hungry to make more money (and if you've come this far, you should be hungry) then you certainly won't fail to find another income stream for lack of options: there are a ton of things you can do to make a quick buck – or even a quick thousand bucks. You just need to be willing to put in the work.

This Action Step is a little different from the others.

Think of this as a choose-your-own-adventure game for your income. Rather than tell you to follow one specific set of steps to make more money, I'm going to lay out a series of options, each with several recommended steps for you to take if it sounds appealing to you.

Not all of these options are going to work for you: some may be too much of a time commitment, and others might not sound like they're worth the money. But the first step is to consider the options. They'll always be right here, waiting for you to give them a shot.

I recommend that you read this chapter beginning to end, then go back and decide which of the income options you'd like to try out first. After you've explored first options, you can try others if it makes sense.

NOTE: In the spirit of brutal honesty, I admit that organizing this section has been a challenge for me. I've seen people struggle with some of these methods, and in those cases I went into great detail to help you avoid common pitfalls. For less complex methods, I just provide the basic need-to-knows. Don't worry about absorbing all the details in your first pass through. Skimming is encouraged.

Sell Everything You Don't Use Regularly

One of the quickest ways to make some money fast is to sell all the random stuff you own and don't use regularly. The average home is a treasure chest of items just waiting to be traded for cash – you wouldn't believe the things that sell successfully on Craigslist or eBay. An old mattress? Yup. Old sheets? Sure. Your old pajamas? Maybe – give it a shot.

Remember, anything you sell now can be replaced later. The opportunity cost of holding on to your fancy watch or earrings is even more than the value of the cash you'd get from selling it.

The true opportunity cost of holding on to expensive things when you have debt = the money you could have saved by A) putting the money from the sale towards your debt, plus B) the money you would have saved by paying less in interest fees. Don't forget that the more you pay down your debt, the lower your interest fees will be (since interest fees are calculated as a percentage of your debt).

Over the course of paying off all your debt, the value of selling your watch for $200 could turn into $500 after factoring in the saved money from would-have-been interest fees. Seriously. Your expensive things are just that: expensive. Far better to sell them now and replace them later when you aren't paying interest on debt.

1. Take an inventory of your household items.

To sell your stuff, you need to know what you have available to sell. Just use a pen and paper for this, no need to get fancy unless you want to. This doesn't have to be comprehensive. Just make sure you nail down the big-ticket items like furniture, appliances, and electronics. Also, include any clothes, artwork, and jewelry you're willing to part with. If you own a lot of stuff, don't bother creating a complete inventory: just list out the things you're willing to consider selling for the right price.

2. Sort items into proper categories.

Either on paper or physically in your home, arrange items into categories (e.g., furniture, appliances, electronics, clothes, jewelry) to better track your wares and make it easier to sell them later.

3. Confirm what you are willing to part with.

Now it's time to make a final decision. Sell? Or keep? Go through the list and confirm what you are willing to part with for now. Remember, this doesn't have to be forever. You can always buy things again later. But also consider this. For each item on the list, think about your Debt Freedom Purpose and ask yourself one question: will it make you happier to have the "thing"? Or would you be happier taking another step towards debt freedom?

4. Take pictures of everything you want to sell.

Now that you've decided on what to sell, it's time to make your products presentable and capture them on camera. People buy with their eyes and you want to make your inventory as attractive as you can. Find a plain background, turn on the lights, and snap pictures of your products individually.

Start with 2-3 pictures of each product: one from the front, one from the side, and one from the rear. Use best judgment to determine the angle of taking the pictures, but try to think about it from the buyer's perspective: what would they want to see? Some products might warrant more than 3 pictures, especially if they're more expensive items. For instance, for a high definition TV you might take a picture from the front with the screen off (showing the glass screen), another picture from the the front with the screen on (showing it's working), a picture from both sides, and a picture of the backside with the connecting ports and plug ins.

5. Choose an online marketplace to sell your stuff.

Start with Craigslist or eBay. Craigslist is best if you'd rather not deal with packaging and shipping items. eBay is best if you're OK with packaging/shipping items and you'd like to receive payment online. You can Google other options as well. There are plenty of sites out there for selling household items.

6. Price your products.

The quickest way to do this is to look at the competition. What are similar items going for on the site? Look at a few related products to get a sense of the price range, then make a judgment call to pick your price. Use quality, condition, features, and date of original purchase (newer = better) as factors for gauging how to price your product.

7. For each product, write a descriptive title.

Highlight one or two key selling points (e.g., "Flat screen", "High Def") while keeping it short and sweet. Someone should be able to scan a page, notice your product, and understand exactly what it is. Look at other related listings to get ideas for your title.

8. For each product, write a clear and concise description.

I highly recommend reading a handful of other product descriptions before you attempt your own. Once you have an idea of what a bad description looks like, it's much easier to write a good one. Common characteristics of a good description include:

- A short and clear description of the product
- A bullet point list of features or positive attributes
- If necessary, an explanation for why you are selling it (e.g., moving out of country, trying to pay off debt, etc.)

9. Post your products and await inquiries!

Try to be quick in responding to messages from your prospective customers. It's common for buyers to inquire about a dozen or more products when shopping for their future couch or TV – the buyer doesn't expect to hear back from everyone, so the "shotgun method" of researching options is common. If you respond first, or quickly, you're much more likely to engage an interested buyer.

10. Negotiate.

The reality is that many people shopping for used products are bargain hunters. They want a good deal. It's more than likely that whatever products you're offering are also being offered by many other sellers, so bargain hunters may push a little to see if you'll lower the price to win their business.

Don't worry – there are plenty of buyers out there, so if the first handful ask for a reduced price that you can't stomach, just politely decline and wait for a more reasonable offer. Keep track of the offers you receive. If you notice a trend of everyone asking for a lower price, consider lowering it.

11. Sell!

Once you have a prospective buyer that you're comfortable with, plan to make the transaction. Take a cash payment if you're selling on Craigslist (I wouldn't recommend accepting a check in case it bounces).

You'll need to arrange a meeting place to exchange the goods for cash. You can schedule the meeting at a public place if you prefer, or just meet outside your home.

If you're selling on eBay, you can accept payment straight through the online platform. Providing the goods is as easy as shipping the product directly to the customer. For smaller items, you can usually just go down to FedEx (or your local shipper) and have them box it up and send it for a small fee.

Negotiate a Raise at Work

Successfully getting a raise depends on many factors, but if the timing is right and you pull it off, this can be a huge boost to your income. Remember the 80/20 rule: one big victory can be worth five smaller ones.

Spend 5 hours researching and planning a conversation with your boss for a $5,000 raise, and you just netted a cool $1,000/hour – more, if you stay with the company for longer than a year.

Before you start down this path, it's important to think about the timing of your request for increased compensation. Do you have a performance review coming up? If so, then it may be best to work hard now and wait for the review to bring this up.

Have you recently had a big "win" at the company? Like successfully completing a big project or bringing in a big client? If so, then bringing this up now while your boss appreciates your recently-highlighted value might make sense.

In an ideal world, you would have a scheduled performance and compensation review every 3 to 6 months – this would give you regular opportunities to check-in with your boss on your performance and make sure you're on the right path.

But while a scheduled and expected meeting is preferred, sometimes you just need to make things happen on your own. Either way, use your best judgment and don't be hasty. It's better to delay your raise than lose your job.

1. Figure out your value to the company.

Before approaching your boss about a raise, you need to know your value to the company. While it's typically not possible to know exactly how valuable you are in terms of a dollar figure, you can cobble together an idea that is 1 part quantitative, 2 parts qualitative.

First, consider your salary + benefits. What are they paying you? Are they contributing to your 401(k)? How much paid time off do you get? Don't worry about getting an exact dollar figure for all this, just be aware of what they provide. The more they provide, the more they appear to value you and your contribution to the company.

Second, identify your value in the marketplace. Go to Glassdoor.com or Salary.com to get the salary range for your job function in your city. If you are in the middle or lower end of the range, you can use this data as leverage to try to get to the higher end. If you're on the higher end, see if there's another related job function you can search for that includes your job's responsibilities. There are usually several similar job titles you can consider.

Third, consider the prospects for someone with your skillset by going to the Occupational Outlook Handbook website from the Bureau of Labor Statistics. Look through the Occupation Finder or search on the website to find something close to your profession. Once you find a match, you can dig in to find the median pay (by most recent year) and the job outlook (higher is better). If your job is in demand, you'll see a "Faster than average" note in this section.

2. Create a "Things I've Done for the Company" list.

This should be a semi-comprehensive list of everything you've done – from joining the company to the present – to help the company advance its interests. That includes activities to increase company revenue, improve employee morale, reduce employee turnover, increase customer loyalty, improve business operations, improve the quality of the product or service, etc.

If you have a task management system or a work log that documents tasks and projects, you can use that as a starting point for filling out this list. The key here is to keep things as tangible as possible. How many star employees have you hired? How many accounts have you closed? How much revenue have you brought into the company? You get the idea.

3. Get a sense for the current state of the company and your department.

To present a compelling argument in favor of increasing your income, you need to have an accurate understanding of how your company is doing and how your department is performing.

Is your company profitable? Is it doing better than last year? How is your company doing relative to the industry? Ask around the office, Google your company's name + "news", and see what you can find out. It will be easier to ask for more money if things are going well.

And how about the department? Does leadership respect your group? Does your boss recognize the value your team provides? It may be difficult to ask for more compensation when the department has not been meeting expectations.

4. Consider the wants and needs of your boss.

This is the person to whom you'll be making your case for a raise, so it's important you understand as much as possible about your boss. What drives him/her? Why does your boss work here? Are you on good terms with your boss? Have they ever confided in you? What are your success metrics? Have you met or exceeded your boss's expectations for your role? What have you done to make your boss's job easier?

5. Prepare your pitch.

If, based on the last two steps, you think it's appropriate to bring up the topic of a raise with your boss, then it's now time to prepare your pitch. The "wing it" method of getting a raise rarely works, and when it does, it's usually just good timing. It's far better to prepare in advance and demonstrate that you take this matter seriously.

Everyone's pitch is going to be different, but consider the following factors:
- Your job performance history
- The biggest, specific pieces of value you've brought to the team and company
- What short anecdotes or stories you can tell that demonstrate your value to the company
- How your salary compares to the average for your market
- What your boss wants
- Potential objections from your boss

6. Schedule the meeting.

Depending on your company's policies, you may already have a process for handling compensation and performance reviews. If you don't, or if the next discussion is some ways out, then you'll need to schedule time to speak with your boss.

Don't blindside your boss by confronting him/her in the hallway with a request to talk compensation. Surprise is not in your favor when you need your boss to be on your side, especially when it comes to compensation.

Instead, politely request a meeting to review your performance and compensation. If they look alarmed or concerned, make it clear that there is no cause for worry, you just want to make sure you're doing a good job.

7. Negotiate a compensation increase.

Now that you've made it to the big meeting, it's time to deliver your pitch. There are a few ways that this conversation could play out, but if you've done your homework during the preceding steps, you should have a good idea of what you can talk about.

Here's an example conversation for how things could go down:

YOU: Thank you for taking the time to speak with me about this, I really appreciate it.

THEM: Of course. So, what do you want to discuss?

YOU: I'd like to talk about my performance at the company. How do you think I'm doing?

THEM: You're doing a good job. I want you to keep it up. Your dah de dah numbers are a little low, but overall you've done solid work. How do you think you're doing?

YOU: I think my hard work and dedication is paying off. As you probably recall, I did… [examples of value you've brought to the company. Remember: always come prepared! It pays to do your homework – literally].

Part of the reason I wanted to have this conversation was to discuss my compensation. Based on the research I've done – and I'd be happy to share the data with you – I've found that… [data from your research indicating you could be paid more].

THEM: [Objections] You haven't been here that long…

YOU: [Thoughtfully address objections] I totally understand this, but I'd ask you to think of this as an investment…

THEM: [More objections] I'm not sure we have the money for this…

YOU: [Continue to thoughtfully address objections] I'm *really* excited to be working here, I just want to be sure that my compensation reflects the value I bring to the company. I know I'm adding a ton of value and I want to find a number that is fair for both of us.

THEM: Well. You make some good points. I'll have to think about it and get back to you.

YOU: Thank you, I hope we can come to an agreement on this.

Here are three common outcomes after having the big meeting, along with how you can handle them.

Outcome #1

Your boss recognizes the value you bring to the company, sees your request as fair, and has the ability to give you a raise – you get a raise.

How to handle it:
Congrats! You got the raise. You worked hard, your boss recognized your value, and was able to give you more money. Don't gloat, don't get overexcited, just be grateful – and while you're at it, talk with your boss and identify specific goals for the next six months. Once you agree on these goals, schedule a follow up performance review for the end of this time period.

This opens the door to future compensation conversations should your performance be rock star status.

Outcome #2
Your boss recognizes the value you bring to the company, sees your request as fair, but does not have the ability to give you a raise – you do not get a raise.

How to handle it:
So things didn't go quite as planned. That's OK. If you sincerely believe your boss recognizes your value and appreciates your work, then maybe it's just timing (hint: it's usually not, but either way you got a "no"). Ask your boss, "when would be a good time to revisit this?" You might propose a follow up meeting six months out.

Depending on your career goals, performance, and satisfaction with your current role at this company, this may be the time to secretly begin feeling out other opportunities outside the company, be it a side gig or changing jobs entirely (more on that in a little).

Outcome #3
Your boss does not recognize the value you bring to the company – you do not get a raise.

How to handle it:
This is the worst-case scenario, but it happens. If you get the idea that your boss does not recognize your value at the company, then you're in trouble. The first people to lose their jobs in layoffs are typically those seen as least valuable to the company.

If your boss doesn't appreciate your work, then you are on shaky ground and should seriously consider changing teams, or jumping ship entirely and joining a different company.

A solid plan of action would involve two paths in parallel: A) Working to improve your image and be seen as a valuable member of the team, and B) Feeling out other job opportunities in case plan A doesn't pan out.

PRO TIP: Sleep on any big career-related decision before you pull the trigger on it. It's easy to get carried away in the heat of the moment – after negotiating with your boss, or after getting a less than desired outcome – so it's important to give your brain time to process everything before you jump to a new course of action. Calm, cool, and collected: the state of mind you want to have for any major decision.

Get a New Job

Switching from one company to another can be a great way to leapfrog your salary quickly into the stratosphere. Long gone are the days of decades upon decades committed to a single employer. We live in a time where employers expect their employees to stick around for as long as it suits them.

Getting a new job doesn't have to be a scary ordeal. And you don't have to commit yourself fully to the process either. You can simply look at this as a potential path for increasing your income.

For many people, the process of getting a new job requires a few steps:

- Figuring out what companies or jobs you'd be interested in exploring
- Updating your resume and LinkedIn profile to make you look appealing for specific roles
- Looking for job openings at companies you're interested in
- Talking with people who work at those companies to better understand the opportunities
- Scheduling interviews with recruiters and hiring managers
- Completing applications
- Preparing for interviews
- Doing interviews
- Having follow up calls and interviews
- Negotiating the compensation package

The full process is beyond the scope of this book, but there are two key areas I want to make sure you are rock solid on:

1. Your ability to source new opportunities
2. Your ability to manage your impression

Rather than having to go skim Craigslist and job boards looking for the diamonds in the rough, what if new opportunities for making money (whether it's a full-time job or something else), came to you?

Over the past five years I've worked 7+ jobs in a variety of industries and job roles, and almost all of them have been sourced through my network – not by going through any formal application process.

Here's a good example.

When I graduated college on the west coast, I moved to the east coast to start a job as an intern at a tech startup.

When I arrived in Boston, I knew no one. I had no connections, no friends, no contacts.

But I knew the importance of having a strong network, so I set about changing that. I attended conferences and events related to my industry. I networked with entrepreneurs and ambitious young professionals, making sure to connect with people at more than a surface level, and to always exchange contact info when I felt a real connection had been made.

PRO TIP: Use Meetup.com, LinkedIn Groups, your local city calendar, and any local event sites (in Boston we have Greenhorn Connect and VentureFizz) to find free or affordable networking opportunities.

Within a year I'd built a strong network, but more importantly, I'd developed relationships with people who supported my growth, both on an individual and professional level. The latter turned out to be pretty important.

At this point I was now managing a 16-person remote team at my company. I had helped the company scale across the country, and I was proud of my accomplishments.

I was walking to the office on a sunny morning in Boston when I got a call from one of my direct reports in NYC. She was hysterical. At first what she said didn't make any sense: executives showing up out of the blue, closing the office, people needing to move to another state, coworkers packing up boxes... I gathered that something big was going on, but I still wasn't prepared for what I was going to see when I entered the office.

As soon as I entered the building, I found a mass exodus of my friends and colleagues, all of them carrying boxes of their stuff and walking out.

It was a mass layoff.

I sat down at my desk, stunned. Until my phone rang and the executive on the other end asked me to meet him in a conference room. Numb, I walked into the room to find the executive standing with a recruiter from HR, the same person who'd hired me over a year ago.

The recruiter looked upset. The executive looked tired.

A polite and respectful conversation followed where I was informed that I had automated myself out of a job, and that unfortunately, there was no room for me somewhere else. I left the meeting with two weeks' severance pay, packed up my things, said some shaky goodbyes, and left the building.

I was devastated.

I'd worked 7 days a week for over a year for this company. I'd been promised stock options which never materialized, raises that were always delayed, and I'd sacrificed most of my social life to put more hours in at the office.

Being my first job out of college, I thought it would be a black mark that I'd been laid off. Who would want to hire a BA in psych who was let go from his first real job?

I'd had a low salary and my savings account was empty, leaving me with two weeks' worth of living (the severance check) until I needed to be earning money again. This put me under a HUGE amount of stress, and I didn't delay in getting started with my job hunt. I figured that getting a good job in two weeks would be near impossible – lucky for me, I was wrong.

Leveraging my network, I began reaching out to my contacts to feel out if there were any opportunities worth exploring.

The day after being laid off, I was connected with a handful of hiring managers via my network, but most valuable of all, a C-suite exec in my network floated my resume internally and within days I was fielding interviews at the company's offices.

One week after being laid off, I was employed as a project manager working for – get this – the partner company of my former employer.

The best part?

I was given a raise over my previous compensation and was put in charge of managing the relationship with my former employer. Within weeks I was back at my former employer's office building to discuss how our companies were working together... only this time I was sitting on the opposite side of the table.

The irony made for some good laughs. But the best part was being employed again, doing something I wanted to do, and making decent money doing it. I'd gone from laid off to gainfully employed in one week, all thanks to my network.

This wasn't a fluke. Since then I've worked for 7+ companies in a variety of roles, with the clear majority of these opportunities coming directly from my network. The phrase "it's not what you know, it's who you know" is often used by people who are struggling to get ahead in their career. It's an excuse for their failure to advance, or their inability to get the promotion they're after.

You however, can use this aphorism as a strategy for success.

It's not fool-proof, it's not a magic bullet that will get you whatever job you want whenever you want it, but if you invest a little time and energy in building this system, you can develop an inbound, passive opportunity stream that will feed you new opportunities for you to choose from.

Build a Passive Opportunity Stream

1. Improve your online impression.

To build a strong, passive opportunity stream that regularly provides you with new income opportunities, you're going to need to develop your network, and to do that, you need to actively manage your online impression.

You probably already do this to some extent: adding new job experience to your LinkedIn profile, updating Facebook, Instagram or Twitter with posts and pictures – but now you need to do this with a specific goal in mind.

Rather than simply "look good" online, you need to carefully craft an impression that elicits the desired result: someone offering you an opportunity that you can seize.

The ultimate online impression trifecta consists of the following:
- Your LinkedIn profile
- Your Twitter page (or other channel relevant to target industry)
- Your personal website

You can get by with one or two of these three, but all three will combine to make a much more powerful impression with a potential recruiter (or the contact who may refer you to a recruiter).

The best way to create amazing profiles on these three platforms is to start by looking for good examples from colleagues, friends, and acquaintances. Just as we learn to speak our native tongue first through imitation, you can look to the pros for inspiration. There's no shame in copying good work. Apple does it. Microsoft does it too.

Knowledge builds on itself through imitation, inspiration, and straight up plagiarism. One of my best resume templates is based on a resume I received when I was in a hiring position.

As you're working on these online pages, pay careful attention to the image you're crafting.

Most people aren't going to read your page in-depth, they're just going to skim it. If you want someone to take away one thing about you, what would it be? That you're a scrappy startup marketer? That you're a charismatic natural-born salesperson?

Don't clutter your pages with text. Be concise, tangible, and avoid using buzzwords.

2. Improve your offline impression.

Making a good online impression is the first step, but you need to be able to follow through with a consistent offline impression when you meet someone in person. This includes everything from how you dress, your body language, the words you use, the stories you tell, and the questions you ask.

The entirety of this step is beyond the scope of this book, but consider some basic questions:

Have you done your homework so you can ask insightful questions?

Do you look more like an engineer (t-shirt, light jeans, sneakers) or a salesperson (button down, dark jeans, loafers)?

Do you have anecdotes in your back pocket that you can whip out when appropriate to pique the person's interest?

Successful people seem to be able to come up with charming stories off the top of their head, but in reality, these stories have been rehearsed and told many times over until they're polished and compelling.

Do you know the language of your industry or market? Specialized fields and industries tend to have lingo specific to that area.

3. Proactively engage people online.

Now that you've crafted a winning impression it's time to start building your network. Your network building arsenal includes online and offline tools – let's start with the digital world.

LinkedIn is a powerful and quick way to engage people professionally. Use the InMail messaging tool to target people you read about in the news, people who work for the company you're interested in, or people who have the job function you want.

You can use the shotgun approach here without repercussions since no one can see how many InMails you're sending, but don't expect a response if you don't personalize your message.

While InMail isn't free, you'll get your InMail messages returned to you to use again if you don't get a response.

Twitter is also an effective means of reaching people, though your response rate may be lower depending on your industry and the job function you're targeting. Tweeting at people out of the blue is totally fine for starting a conversation, but if that person goes to your page and sees that all you're doing is tweeting directly at people... that won't look good.

Use this tool selectively, and don't spam – people can see how often you're messaging others and your target contacts won't feel special if they appear to be just another in a long line of random reach outs.

The goal of your InMails and tweets is to engage interesting, ambitious, successful people and to get on the phone with them or take them out to coffee or lunch.

Keep your messages short and sweet.

On LinkedIn I typically say something like, "Hi <Name>, noticed you <interesting thing about them> and I wanted to get in touch. I <thing you both have in common> and would love to talk with you about <topic>. Can I buy you a cup of coffee?"

On Twitter I'll keep it even shorter (due to the 144-character limit): "Hey @Name, awesome that you're <interesting thing they're doing>. Would love to talk about <topic>. Can we chat?"

Before doing these reach outs, make sure you have a tangible reason for wanting to talk. Busy people don't accept meetings with strangers just because "we should talk." If you do your homework on the person, read their personal blog, learn about their company, and anticipate their desires, you'll have no problem finding something that will pique their interest.

4. Proactively engage people offline or on the phone.

Now that you've managed to get someone to take your call or meet with you in person, it's time to build a relationship.

You could approach this in a scammy, salesy way, and try to get something out of them right off the bat, but this won't help you in the long-term. Instead, try to connect with them on a meaningful level and get to know the person. This won't necessarily pay dividends right away, but as you continue this process, you'll end up with a strong network of real relationships.

Whether you're talking with someone in person or on the phone, the conversation should be about them. This sounds strange, given that your goal is to have them help you, but remember: you're not looking to extract value just yet, in fact, your goal is to add value.

Try to keep them talking as much as possible. Find things about them that you can be genuinely interested in. The more interested in them you are, the more interested in you they will become. People feel good talking about themselves.

If you ask for their help, their advice, their wisdom, they'll feel appreciated and in turn want to help you. We all have a natural inclination to help others and you can use this as a stepping stone to building a more meaningful relationship.

One of the most important takeaways from this conversation should be figuring out how can I help this person? If you know what they want, their goals, their ambitions, their passions, you can more easily build a relationship by helping them (see next step).

End every conversation with an open door to future conversations. You can do this by asking something like, "I really appreciate you taking the time today – seriously, thank you. Would it be alright if I follow up with you in the not too distant future in case I have more questions?"

Your first meeting is not the time to show off or try to look good. Leave your ego behind and focus on making them feel valued.

5. Add value, add value, add value.

Now that you've established the initial relationship, it's time to strengthen it. It is STILL not time to ask for anything. No asking for job offers, referrals or connections. You need to play the Godfather card and give them something without any request for them to return the favor. By doing so, you'll build up your social capital and they'll be more likely to repay the favor later.

Adding value could consist of:
- Commenting on their blog posts
- Retweeting their tweets
- Giving thoughtful feedback on their LinkedIn posts
- Introducing them to people they'd like to speak with
- Sending business their way
- Mentioning them online as great person to talk to about X

6. Make your "ask."

Only after adding 3 or more tangible pieces of value should you begin to consider how to make a request from your new relationship.

You can do this directly by emailing him/her with a specific request.

"Hey <Name>, would you mind introducing me to the person who handles inbound marketing at your company? I'd love to talk with them about what they're working on and see if I might be able to help."

Or even better, don't cash in your chips with a direct request, and instead just float a casual idea onto their radar.

"Hey <Name>, just FYI - I'm on the job hunt and looking for fast-paced tech companies that need marketing help. If you come across anything, please keep me in mind!"

7. Pay upkeep to your network.

If you commit to meeting just one new interesting person per week, within months you'll have established a powerful network of meaningful connections. But just like owning a boat, or any other powerful vehicle, this ownership comes with a cost: your social network maintenance fee.

Your new relationships will last much longer thanks to your careful development process, but they'll still weaken over time. People will forget what you do, what your strengths are, or how charismatic or charming you are.

You have to pay upkeep to your network by continuing to dish out the value.

Step 7 never ends.

You'll need to continue adding value consistently over time to keep your relationships strong. This doesn't mean you must add value every week, or even every month, but a good touch point once every 2-3 months is a decent standard for maintaining a healthy relationship. The more important the relationship, the more touch points (or at least, the more valuable the touch point) you should strive for.

The enormous benefit to having a strong network is not only the ability to ask for favors, but the increased likelihood of receiving new ideas, knowledge, and opportunities from people. People like to share good things with other people they like and your contacts will be far more likely to share new opportunities with you if you consistently add value to them. It's basic reciprocity, and it's something all human beings are biologically compelled to participate in.

Job Hunting with a Sniper Rifle

While having a way to source new opportunities in general is a good thing, perhaps you have a very specific job or company you want to go after – and you don't have time to wait for your network to provide an "in." In this case, it's time to pull out your sniper rifle and take aim using a careful process that is 2 parts detective work, 1 part impression management.

To get a specific job, or work for a specific company, you need to get your foot in the door – to find a way to start a conversation that will lead to a job offer.

You also need to talk to the right people. You could be the best marketer in the world for a company but if you're chatting up the Director of Engineering they probably won't appreciate your creative brilliance.

We've already talked about ways to manage your impression in the last section, so for this objective I'm going to assume you know enough to do your homework and make sure your impression aligns with the interests of whichever person or company you're targeting.

1. Choose your target.

Is there a specific company you want to work for? A specific job you want? Both? Figure out what you're going after and make a commitment to invest a few hours or more per week to giving it a shot. If you know what type of job you want, go find a company that's hiring for it. If you know what company you want, pick a job to target.

Whether you're more focused on the role or the company, you need to end up with a specific company to target. You can target multiple companies eventually, but you need to start with one.

PRO TIP: Don't worry if you're not sure exactly what you want to do at the company just yet. You can figure that out after Step 3.

2. Stalk the crap out of the company.

Now that you have a company in your crosshairs, it's time to stalk the living crap out of them. Go to Google News and read anything you can find about the company. Make note of who is being mentioned in articles, what topics are being discussed, why it's interesting or newsworthy, and when the news happened.

Read the About or Team page on the company site. Look over their News page if they have one to see if you missed anything. Read through other pages to learn more.

By the end of this step, you should know what the company does, what type of customers they serve, a little history about the company, where they are going (what is their vision for the future?), and who the key movers and shakers at the company are (e.g., CEO, co-founders, VPs and directors).

3. Stalk the crap out of a target person.

Now that you have a baseline understanding of the company, you need to stalk the crap out of either A) your potential future boss, or B) a potential internal champion. If you know what job you want, great—look over the job openings and figure out who you would report to. If you don't know exactly what job would be the best fit, or if you're hoping they'll create a position for you, look for someone who might be able to develop a relationship with—an internal champion.

Internal champions are great, because even if they don't have the power to hire you to the company, they can push their colleagues to meet with you, or give you inside information that will allow you to ace the interview. Sounds unfair, I know, but I'm just telling the truth.

Often, companies offer jobs internally before opening them up to the public. Existing employees and the people they know have an unfair advantage because they have access to information that outsiders don't, but you can level the playing field by acquiring an internal champion.

Use the company's website along with LinkedIn to find your target person. LinkedIn has Advanced Search, which will allow you to customize the city, company, job title, etc. in your hunt. If you can't find much, good old fashioned Google searches might reveal something.

Now that you have a specific person you'd like to eventually meet with, it's time to get stalking. I use the term "stalk" jokingly, but in all seriousness, you need to do some real digging (nothing illegal or creepy) to understand this person. Knowledge is power, and the more you know, the more you can turn that knowledge into practical action, whether that means connecting on a deeper level when you meet them in person, or talking about the right things to give a powerful impression.

To stalk effectively, I recommend starting by creating a Google or Word doc where you can track everything you uncover about this person.

Next, find all their online social profiles. You can install Rapportive or HubSpot's Sidekick to use within your Gmail inbox. I currently use Rapportive, and anytime I enter someone's email address into my "To" line, Rapportive auto-populates a sidebar that shows any social profiles it could find associated with the email address, along with some high-level details taken from their LinkedIn profile.

Of course, you'll need their email address to make this work (and to contact them later). I recommend starting with Anymail finder as a quick one-stop shop for getting an email address. It usually works, and you can do 20 verified email searches for free before needing to upgrade to a paid account.

If that doesn't work, (or even if it does) try Better Whois to get some intel on the company, including their email format (e.g., first.last@company.com). Enter the company's URL in the Better Whois search box and wait for it to pull up the results. Usually, you'll get a long list of results back showing detailed information, like the company's contact email address, who created the website, the office address, etc.

Sometimes this information is extremely revealing, other times the company will have taken steps to hide this information and instead of seeing company data, you'll see notes saying it's protected, or you'll see data but it'll be for the domain service they use instead of the company you're researching.

If this search gave you a company email address other than "info@" or something standard like that, then great! You can use the format to guess your target's email address. Try plugging the email into your "To:" line in a new email and see if Rapportive or Sidekick finds anything.

If Better Whois doesn't work, there are a bunch of other "Whois" sites you can try. Google 'em.

As a last-ditch effort, use MailTester to plug in various email address combinations and see if they're valid. Try combinations like first@company.com, firstinitial.lastname@company.com, first.last@company.com, etc. Unless the company has a protected server setup, the service will be able to tell you if the email address is valid or not.

If after all that, you still don't have an email address for your target person, use Salesforce's Data.com (first two contacts are free) or hire someone on Upwork to get you the email address.

OK, you've got an email address, that's good, but you still need to learn about this person. Do some digging and see what you can

find about your target person. Go through their blog, do a Whois lookup on it. Use All My Tweets to see what they tweet about (and possibly what they would be interested in talking about).

Do they have an Instagram account? What do they take pictures of? Are they listed on the company website? What does their bio say about them? Check out their LinkedIn profile. Where have they worked? Have they stayed in one industry? Danced around a bit? Have they stayed in one discipline or tried a variety of roles? How long have they been at the company? Do they have endorsements or recommendations?

Write down as much as you can and highlight anything noteworthy.

PRO TIP: Always look for common ground opportunities. Shared interests, passions, or experiences are all great for finding a meaningful way to connect with someone on a deeper level.

4. Acquire a mutual connection. (Optional but recommended)

Meeting someone who knows your target person is a powerful way to gain additional intel, as well as to potentially develop an ally who can rep you. This person might end up being an internal champion, but doesn't have to be. The goal is to feel out the company and your target person before meeting him or her face to face. You might already have a shared connection (check LinkedIn), but if you don't, see if you can find someone who works in the same department, or is at a similar level within the company. You can typically find good adjacent connections on LinkedIn, but the company's Team page is another resource.

Meet this person for coffee or lunch if possible. Your reason might be "to talk with them about opportunities at the company in their department" or to "talk with them about their role and get their advice."

At some point in the conversation, bring up the target person. See what they say about him/her. Depending on the relationship they have, you may be able to get an introduction via the person you're speaking with.

5. Arrange a meeting with your target person.

In an ideal world, you'd be able to get an email introduction to your target person via another person at the same company, or by a trusted friend of the person. This can't always happen, but step 4 may have enabled this. If not, a cold email is your next best bet.

Keep this email short and to the point. Also, be polite, and craft a compelling hook to get their attention. Mention something you discovered from steps 1 or 2. This will let them know you're seriously interested in talking with them, that you've done your homework, and that you're not just emailing a ton of people in the hope that a couple will respond (shotgun approach).

Your goal is to get an in-person meeting (be it at their offices, out for lunch, coffee, in an underground bunker), but your fallback is a phone call. Start with the big ask, retreat to the little ask if necessary.

6. Pique their interest.

We've already talked about how to improve your online and offline impression, but keep in mind that the goal of this first conversation is to pique their interest. If you don't have their attention, then nothing else matters.

Your weapons are quick anecdotes and stories that illustrate your accomplishments without getting too braggy.

You should be ready to handle questions about your experience, your motivations, your mission in life. You should know what motivates them, what experiences they've been through, and their mission in life. Find common ground quickly, but never lie. Stretching the truth is one thing ("I love Malcolm Gladwell too") but lying is never a good long-term strategy ("Malcolm Gladwell and I play Pokemon Go together on the weekends").

7. Move in for the kill.

Once you've piqued their interest, it's time aim for the bullseye and pull the trigger. You need to get this person on your side and take a firm step forward towards getting a job. If you're speaking with a potential internal champion, focus on representing your value well, and ask about opportunities to work at the company. See if they have any recommendations for how you might talk with your target person, or how you might get the job you're interested in. If you're talking with your potential future boss, be clear and directly express your interest in working for them.

You should already understand the company as well as your target person at this point, which should give you all the talking points you need, but remember to avoid buzzwords and focus on expressing how you can add value to the company/team in tangible terms.

You can find all the tools mentioned in this section at www.debtdestroyerbook.com/tools.

Your Money Making Toolkit

I scanned the handful of screenshots, names of the key actors, and quickly threw together a title: "Pamela Likes to Get Naked Outside." I'd just made $0.25. On to the next one. I never thought I'd be naming porn titles to make money, but it was easy, didn't require much brain power, and hell – I was desperate for every extra penny I could get my hands on.

Using Amazon's Mechanical Turk, now known as Mturk, I quickly ran through tasks to make quick money. It wasn't anything I'd get rich doing, but across a handful of tasks, the quarters added up. Whenever I was ready, I could transfer the funds to my bank account, and bam — another handful of bucks to throw at my debt.

Not all my endeavors were quite so lewd or paid so little.

I hit the jackpot when I discovered that in many states you do not need a real estate license to sell a business. You need a license if you're selling real estate in addition to the business, but if you're only selling the business, many states will let anyone act as a broker.

Typical business brokers charge 10-12% of the total sale value for their services, so as a new broker (well, that's what I called myself), I charged half that. The great thing with selling people someone's business is that there's very little downside for the seller. If you find them a buyer, great. If you don't, no skin off their back.

As a broker, you're working for commission, so it's up to you to make the work worth it.

This unique financial arrangement — typical in some industries, unheard of in others — allowed me to have a shot at making serious money, and it paid off.

I sold a restaurant in Boston and walked away with a check for $5,000.

The work required for the payout? Posting two advertisements (one for each restaurant I was trying to sell) and emailing a handful of local restaurant owners.

I had to pay $500 total for the two ads, which means my ROI was 900%. It took a few months for the deal to close, but my involvement was minimal, which meant I could continue to do my full-time job and side gigs in parallel.

There are many ways to make some side income and we're going to look at a good handful of them. This might be a bit overwhelming, so if you feel like this is all too much just take a deep breath and remember that these are all just options.

To make these earning opportunities easier to digest, I created a simple scoring system that highlights some of the key things to consider.

Intensity Level = How much effort does this require?
(1 = low, 5 = high)

Crazy Rating = How far outside the "average" comfort zone is this?
(Normal, Unconventional, Tin Foil Hat)

Earnings Estimate = Ballpark estimate of how much you'll earn
($ = low earnings, $$$$$ = high earnings)

Pick one or two of these to explore further and leave the rest for later:

Participate in research studies
Schools and institutions alike commonly run studies to better understand people with certain conditions/characteristics.
- Intensity Level: 2
- Crazy Rating: Unconventional
- Earnings Estimate: $$

Review music for cash
Listen to music and get paid. Quick and easy to get started.
- Intensity Level: 1
- Crazy Rating: Normal
- Earnings Estimate: $

Test websites
Test out a new website, fill out a survey, get paid.
- Intensity Level: 1
- Crazy Rating: Normal
- Earnings Estimate: $

Do side-jobs online
Sign up for Upwork, Freelancer, and TaskRabbit and start doing jobs to make money fast. Don't just wait for work to come to you, apply for jobs and reach out to people. Explain why you're qualified and ask for referrals.
- Intensity Level: 3
- Crazy Rating: Normal
- Earnings Estimate: $$$

Be someone's friend
A totally legal service where you hang out with someone and get paid. You might go to a restaurant or movie, or could join someone for a dinner party.
- Intensity Level: 3
- Crazy Rating: Tin Foil Hat
- Earnings Estimate: $$

Sell your body's renewable resources
You can sometimes sell plasma for $20 to $50.
- Intensity Level: 2
- Crazy Rating: Unconventional
- Earnings Estimate: $$

Sell your sperm
You can typically sell sperm for $30-200.
- Intensity Level: 2
- Crazy Rating: Unconventional
- Earnings Estimate: $$$

Sell your eggs
It's a process, but women can often sell their eggs for anywhere from $5,000 to $10,000.
- Intensity Level: 5
- Crazy Rating: Unconventional
- Earnings Estimate: $$$$$

Sell your fecal matter
Sell your feces for $40 a pop.
- Intensity Level: 3
- Crazy Rating: Tin Foil Hat
- Earnings Estimate: $$

Do random gigs online
Sign up for Fiverr where you might write a description, create a graphic, or translate something. There are a variety of job types.
- Intensity Level: 2
- Crazy Rating: Normal
- Earnings Estimate: $$

Cook for guests in your home
Like to cook? Sign up for EatWith to host small dinner parties and get paid a rate per guest.
- Intensity Level: 3
- Crazy Rating: Unconventional
- Earnings Estimate: $$

Join a promotional company
Promo-events, distributing flyers, some of these jobs can be lame but the money isn't bad for a few hours spent over the weekend.
- Intensity Level: 4
- Crazy Rating: Unconventional
- Earnings Estimate: $$

Become a mystery shopper
Go undercover and fill out questionnaires.

- Intensity Level: 2
- Crazy Rating: Normal
- Earnings Estimate: $

Teach a language online.
Sign up for Italki and teach a language for money.
- Intensity Level: 3
- Crazy Rating: Unconventional
- Earnings Estimate: $$

Teach a class online
If you're particularly good at something you can sign up for Skillshare and Udemy and create a paid class. You don't need to be an expert. You just need to know more than someone else.
- Intensity Level: 3
- Crazy Rating: Unconventional
- Earnings Estimate: $$

Drive for a ridesharing service like Uber
Have a car? Start making money during down time. It's super easy to start and you get to meet interesting people while earning income.
- Intensity Level: 2
- Crazy Rating: Normal
- Earnings Estimate: $$$

Consult for businesses
Have business or tech skills? Create a profile on Angel.co and polish up your LinkedIn profile, then start reaching out to local businesses. Offer your services for free to friends and acquaintances to get some quick positive reviews and recommendations. Always ask for referrals!
- Intensity Level: 4
- Crazy Rating: Unconventional
- Earnings Estimate: $$$$$

Get a real-estate license
Like working with people? Get your real-estate license for roughly $200 and you can start working almost immediately. There are tons of real-estate firms you can join, and you can pitch your services to your friends and family to get started.
- Intensity Level: 4
- Crazy Rating: Normal
- Earnings Estimate: $$$$

Become a part time mover
Want to get a workout while getting paid? Become a part time mover and make some cash while lifting things up and putting them down.
- Intensity Level: 5
- Crazy Rating: Unconventional
- Earnings Estimate: $$$

Broker the sale of businesses
Like working with people but don't want to get a license? You can act as a broker to help sell a restaurant or local business without a license as long as it doesn't include land. There are websites like BizBuySell to help you get leads.
- Intensity Level: 3
- Crazy Rating: Unconventional
- Earnings Estimate: $$$$$

Participate in clinical trials
Help science and get paid for it! Make sure the $ is worth it.
- Intensity Level: 2
- Crazy Rating: Tin Foil Hat
- Earnings Estimate: $$

Rent out your place
Sign up on Airbnb to start hosting guests for a nightly rate. Get your friends to review you and make sure to post flattering photos with a detailed description of your place.

- Intensity Level: 3
- Crazy Rating: Unconventional
- Earnings Estimate: $$$$

Get a remote job so you can work from home
Check out RemoteOK.io and Jobspresso.co. Both sites have big lists of remote jobs that are being offered by companies who believe that employees should be able to work from where they want to work. You can sort the job listings by job type to make it easier to find jobs that apply to you.
- Intensity Level: 3
- Crazy Rating: Unconventional
- Earnings Estimate: Variable

To make sure links stay up to date, I've listed all the website links to these opportunities on this page:
www.debtdestroyerbook.com/moneymakingtoolkit

OK I think that's enough for now.

If you want more options, go to the link above and you'll see everything I've got.

We've now reached the end of this book.

There is one more chapter, but I must warn you: it's not for everyone. If you're feeling daring, proceed with caution.

At this point, you should have some serious debt-destroying momentum carrying you forward. Your DFP, public commitment, and quick win should have seen to that. If for whatever reason you do not feel motivated and empowered to pay off your debt, please let me know.

I take this topic very seriously and I appreciate hearing your feedback. You can reach me here:

charlie@debtdestroyerbook.com

If you have a "win", a success story, or any other feedback you want to share, that's awesome too. I read every email.

I wish you good debt destroying,

Charlie

Chapter 11

Sprint or Marathon: A Word of Caution

"Today I will do what others won't, so tomorrow I can accomplish what others can't."
— JERRY RICE

I had just finished Yuval Harari's online Coursera class, "A Brief History of Humankind" which covered the history of homo sapiens from our earliest beginnings through the present and beyond.

It was a great class, full of insightful lectures and entertaining stories. I'd spent countless nights in the office up late on my laptop, watching the videos and reading related material. Now I was finally finished.

And you know what? I couldn't remember any of it.

Four months of 5-hours-per-night sleep had taken its toll, and none of Harari's lectures made it into my long-term memory. My brain wasn't able to encode that much information in my sleep-deprived state.

That wasn't the only cost of my sprint to debt freedom.

During the many days and nights I spent in the office (where else was I going to hang out?), I'd managed to distance myself from more than one close friend.

I remember one evening at the office, a friend drove over to pick me up and take me to a social gathering — but I missed his text message, then tried to buy a few more minutes after I was pulled into a meeting, then lost track of time.

My friend had been patient, but he was doing me a favor: not only giving me a ride, but introducing me to a group of his friends. And here I was 30 minutes late.

That's not something you do to a close friend, but in my sleep-deprived state, I lacked the mental clarity to recognize that I'd been rude.

Since then, I've read Harari's book "Sapiens" to make up for the lost class (which I highly recommend) – but the rift I created in my friendship remains to this day.

For every decision made, something is gained and something is lost. There are real world consequences for your actions and in this final chapter I want to talk about two different approaches to becoming debt free and the pros and cons of each one.

If you follow the steps in this book and commit fully to each one, you WILL achieve debt freedom. Eventually.

The big question of course, is how long will it take.

The Debt Elimination System you created back in Chapter 8 shows you how long it will take to pay off your debt assuming a fixed payment amount (you can play with the numbers to see different outcomes).

But imagine how things could change if you were to cut your living expenses by 30%? Or if you got a side hustle that paid an extra thousand bucks a month?

Your debt freedom journey can change dramatically depending on the effort you put into Chapters 9 and 10.

I want you to think about your debt freedom journey and right now decide on the analogy you will use to visualize your path to freedom.

There are two distinct paths: the sprint and the marathon.

If you read debt blogs or personal finance articles, you'll find that almost all of them compare paying off debt to a marathon. It's a fair analogy, since for most people the journey will be a long one which requires patience, endurance, and resilience.

But for an ambitious and hyper-motivated few, the marathon analogy doesn't quite fit – nor does it inspire the excitement and energy necessary to achieve faster than average results.

For these people, we turn to the sprint analogy.

Now, I'm not opening any of the other Action Steps up for debate, but for this one I will. And that's your Debt Elimination Strategy.

Depending on how much debt you have, how much money you make, and how hard you're willing to work, it's possible for you to fast-track your results and achieve debt freedom in a fraction of the time it would normally take...

IF you are willing to take more extreme measures.

I'm not going to sugar-coat it. This path involves more sacrifice, more willpower, greater attention to habit-building, and a less friendly debt elimination system.

But the reward is a much earlier debt payoff date.

We're about to compare the differences between the "sprint" vs. the "marathon," but you should know that I'm making some semi-arbitrary decisions around income and debt figures and you need to use your best judgment. As with many things in life, the lines are blurred and there are (50) shades of grey, no black and white here.

The Debt Sprint

Remember how I had you organize your debts by smallest balance so that you can tackle the lowest hanging fruit first? Well, as I mentioned before, this isn't the optimal strategy from a financial perspective; it's the optimal strategy from a motivational perspective.

To crank out more financial efficiency, a debt sprint will include the Debt Avalanche method of repayment:

1. Pay the minimums on everything.
2. List your debts by order of interest rate, highest first, lowest last.
3. Put all available funds towards your highest interest rate debt until it's paid off. Then the next highest, and so on.

This method will guarantee you don't waste a penny on interest fees you could have avoided, and those pennies could add up to hundreds of dollars saved by the time you pay off the last debt.

This is the method often recommended by financial advisors.

Recommended Criteria for the Debt Sprint Method

Your Total Debt: $25,000 or less
Your Current Net Cash Flow per Month: $2,000 or more
Cost Cutting: 50%+ reduction during sprint
Income Generation: 50%+ increase during sprint
Repayment Method: Avalanche
Fun Budget: $0

The purpose of doing a debt sprint is to get out of debt as fast as humanly possible by making HUGE lifestyle changes. This option is not recommended for most people. To successfully complete a debt sprint, you'll need to maintain these lifestyle changes (read: sacrifices) for 3-6 months.

Here's an example profile of someone who this might be good for:

Total Debt: $25,000
Take Home Income: $4,000/month
Current Expenses: $2,000/month

And here's what s/he could do to *sprint* to debt freedom:
- Get a consulting or contract job that pays $1,000 a month in take-home
- Drive for Uber, do Upwork jobs, and hustle to make another $1,000 a month in take-home
- Move into the basement of a friend's house to eliminate rent bill
- Buy groceries in bulk, stop drinking, stop going out for dinner
- Only spend money in cash, no credit cards used for duration of sprint

This person would now be making approximately $6,000 per month and about $5,000 of it would go towards debt.

At this rate, all the debt would be eliminated in approximately 5 months. This doesn't account for interest fees, but it gives you an idea of roughly how long the sprint will take.

If you could make even more money, or spend even less, you could accelerate this further. Brokering the sale of one business, or scoring an extra consulting or contract job could bring you down to a 4 or even 3-month sprint.

This is not easy to do.

Not only is this not easy, but it's just not plain possible for some folks. Making a sprint like I've described only makes sense if you can get enough income to justify it, and honestly, five months is a long time to make big sacrifices.

Of course, if you're the type of ambitious, go-getter that thrives on challenge, then what feels like sacrifice to others might feel like adventure to you. (It did for me)

Now let's consider the tried and true method.

The Debt Marathon

To keep you motivated and energized along the path to debt freedom, a debt marathon will include the Debt Snowball method of repayment:

1. Pay the minimums on everything.
2. List your debts by order of balance, lowest first, highest last.
3. Put all available funds towards your lowest balance debt until it's paid off. Then the next lowest, and so on.

This method will guarantee you get small wins along the way, keeping you motivated and giving you a concrete sense of progress.

This is the method most recommended by people who have paid off debt before.

Recommended Criteria for the Debt Marathon Method

Your Total Debt: $25,000 or more
Your Current Net Cash Flow per Month: Any amount
Cost Cutting: 25%+ reduction during marathon
Income Generation: 25%+ increase during marathon
Repayment Method: Snowball
Fun Budget: 5-15% of take-home pay

Here's an example profile of someone who this might be good for:

Total Debt: $75,000
Take Home Income: $2,500/month
Current Expenses: $2,500/month

And here's what s/he could do to *marathon* their way to debt freedom:

- Get a side job that pays $700 a month in take-home
- Drive for Uber, do Upwork jobs, and hustle to make another $300 a month in take-home
- Airbnb a room or entire place out occasionally for extra income
- Move to a cheaper home to save on the rent bill
- Buy groceries in bulk, drink less, go out for dinner 1-2 times a month
- Only spend money in cash, no credit cards used for duration of marathon

This person would now be making approximately $3,500 month. Let's assume they got their costs down by 25% (new expenses = $1,875/month). This means about $1,625 of their income would go towards debt.

In this case, all the debt would be eliminated in about 4.5 years assuming a 6% average interest rate of all debts.

If you're in the marathon boat, this time-frame might sound scary, but the great thing about this plan is that you're still mostly living your regular life while paying off your debt.

Sure, there are some changes you need to make to improve your cash flow, especially if you're currently spending more than you earn, but the marathon method will keep you enjoying life while you're paying off your bills.

The point of the marathon method is to make sustainable cuts in spending and to stay motivated throughout the journey. Your debt probably took a while to accumulate and it's going to take a while to pay off too, but the journey will be worth it.

By having fun and enjoying your life along the way, you'll increase the odds of sticking with your plan and successfully making it to the finish line.

A sprint doesn't require the attention to long-term motivation like a marathon does. You can get away with big sacrifices and big intensity because it's so temporary. But a marathon is long and you absolutely need to pay attention to your long-term motivation.

To simplify your life, I recommend you pick either the debt sprint or the debt marathon and then commit to it 100%.

And if there's even a *shred* of doubt about which plan to go with… the debt marathon is your answer.

This is your life, your money, your legacy. So whatever you do, make the most of it.

Action Steps and Guiding Principles

Action Steps
1. Accept The Debt Challenge
2. Find Your Debt Freedom Purpose
3. Get a Quick Win
4. Make a Public Commitment
5. Create a Debt Tracker
6. Create a Spending Plan
7. Create a Debt Elimination System
8. Prioritize Your Expenses
9. Increase Your Income

Your Guiding Principles
- Celebrate small wins to stay motivated along the way
- Use progressive escalation to start with small steps, then graduate to bigger ones
- Choose "ownership" over "guilt"
- Take action every day to keep momentum going
- Use your limited willpower wisely (focus on the important things)
- Find role models and sources of inspiration to encourage big action

Your Next Step

You've finished the book.

You're on the path of paying off your debt.

What do you do next?

That's where www.DebtDestroyerBook.com/Step1 comes in.

I created this online resource so that you can keep up to date with the latest income hacks, savings tips, and debt destroying strategies out there.

Each week I do a roundup of the best knowledge available on the web and share it with my readers. I also release subscriber-only cheat sheets, step-by-step templates, and other helpful guides to help you pay off debt faster.

I highly recommend you take 60 seconds right now to visit DebtDestroyerBook.com/Step1 and subscribe.

Go to the Link Below to Subscribe Now

www.DebtDestroyerBook.com/step1

It's 100% free, I only send 1-2 emails each week, and you can unsubscribe at any time (I won't be offended).

By joining, you will also receive email alerts when I release new books, and you'll have the chance to get ALL of these new releases for just 99 cents!

Can You Do Me a Favor?

Thanks for checking out my book.

I'm confident that you're well on your way to achieving financial freedom if you follow what's written inside. But before you go, I have one small favor to ask...

Would you take 60 seconds and write a quick blurb about this book on Amazon?

Reviews are the best way for independent authors (like me) to get noticed, sell more books, and continue to spread my message to as many people as possible. I also read every review and use the feedback to write future revisions – and future books, even.

Click here to leave a review on Amazon.com

Note: The above link may not work on certain Kindle devices. If that's the case, please manually navigate to the book's page on Amazon to leave a review.

Thank you – I really appreciate your support.

About the Author

Charlie Johnson is a former startup guy who's on a mission to eradicate debt. He's an online entrepreneur, world traveler, and overall, an extremely impatient person.

Made in the USA
Middletown, DE
27 July 2025